CONTENTS

# THE CHURCH BOOK

ANNE FARNCOMBE

NATIONAL CHRISTIAN EDUCATION COUNCIL
Robert Denholm House
Nutfield, Redhill, Surrey, RH1 4HW

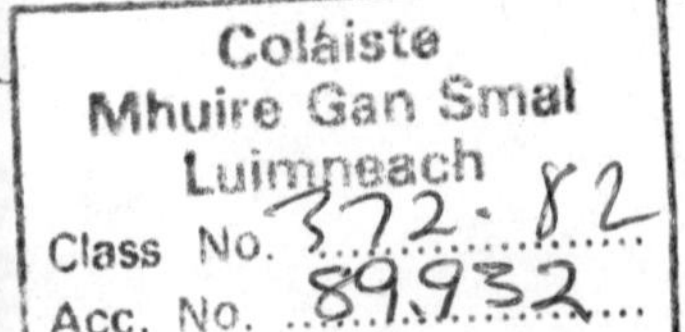


TO JOHN AND RITA

*Other books in this series:*
THE CHRISTMAS BOOK
THE EASTER BOOK

ACKNOWLEDGEMENT
Biblical quotations are from the *Good News Bible* (The Bible Societies/Collins), © American Bible Society, New York, 1976 and are used by permission.

British Library Cataloguing in Publication Data

Farncombe, Anne
The church book.
1. Church — Juvenile literature
I. Title II. National Christian Education Council
260 BV600.2

ISBN 0-7197-0468-5

First published 1988


ISBN 0-7197-0468-5

Typeset by Avonset, Midsomer Norton, Avon
Printed and bound by Page Bros (Norwich) Ltd, Norwich

# THE BEGINNING OF THE CHURCH

Jesus was born a Jew. He grew up in a Jewish family, and belonged to a nation of very religious people who believed that they had been chosen by God.

Jesus studied the Scriptures as all Jewish boys did, and although he came from an ordinary family, he later became a religious teacher, or rabbi. He gathered a small group of disciples round him, which was not unusual in those days in Palestine. There were many such teachers with their groups of followers.

The Jewish people knew that God cared for them, but they were not happy. For hundreds of years they had been ruled by, and despised by, other nations. They longed and waited for a leader who would be able to deliver them from their hardships. This leader would be their *Messiah*. Some thought he would come as a great king; others thought he would be a military man.

FIND AND READ WHAT IS WRITTEN IN THE BOOK OF ISAIAH CHAPTER 9, VERSE 7.

No one guessed that the carpenter's son from Nazareth was the long-awaited Messiah. He was certainly a teacher with great appeal to the people: he promised them love and kindness, healing and comfort, and taught that everyone, not just the Jews — the chosen people — were loved by God. He suggested that there was a day coming when the ancient Jewish laws would be replaced by newer, better ones. The Jewish authorities were not pleased, and regarded him as a threat to the way of life that they had known for centuries.

Moreover, Jesus disapproved of people who put great importance on being rich and powerful. This did not please the Pharisees and other men who held high offices. They despised Jesus, too, for enjoying the company of people who did not fit into society — the drop-outs, outcasts, and those with diseased bodies or minds. Jesus spoke of these people as being accepted and loved by God.

But Jesus' band of followers, the disciples, had learned from his teaching, and crowds of people had listened to his words. When he was arrested and killed they could not understand what had happened.

Then word went round that Jesus had conquered death! He had been seen by many people, a recognisable, living, joyful man.

People began to have fresh hope that this really was the Messiah for whom they had waited so long.

Before Jesus finally left his friends, he gave them some very clear instructions:

(Matthew 28.19-20, GNB)

*Jesus also promised them something. What was it? Read the last sentence of Matthew 28.20.*

At first, the disciples had no idea how they could carry out these commands. They could not even guess at the number of people there were in the Roman world outside Palestine, and were totally ignorant of the countries and people beyond it. They themselves had never travelled far; many of them were uneducated, working men who knew no language except their own. On top of this, they were wanted men, marked by the authorities as dangerous and subversive, a threat to Jewish tradition and worship.

No doubt the disciples met in groups to discuss what they should do. Jesus had told them to go to Jerusalem and wait for the gift of God.

The secret meeting place for the group of friends was a large room built on to one of the flat-roofed houses in the city. There they prayed for guidance and help; they prayed that they might be strong when the time came for them to begin the work Jesus had told them to do.

Jesus' mother, Mary, was with them, and his brothers, and many of the women who had supported the group through difficult times.

The Jewish Festival of Pentecost was being celebrated there, and Jerusalem was milling with people from all over the Jewish world.

On the Day of Pentecost the group met, and something strange yet wonderful seemed to happen.

Read about this in Acts 2.1–4

**God's gift had been given!**

*Pretend the room had been 'bugged' by agents or spies wanting to collect evidence about the group's plans.*

*Write what you think would have been heard from that room.*

The change in all who met in that room was immediate and amazing. Suddenly they were strong and unafraid, excited and determined. They knew what they had to do, and they had the power to do it — without limit. As well as being disciples — learners — they were apostles — messengers.

**The Christian Church, the people of God through Jesus Christ, had begun!**

# THE EARLIEST CHRISTIAN CHURCH

After the events of Pentecost, when the Holy Spirit gave the waiting friends of Jesus the power to do his work, the Church of God had begun.

The excited disciples and other followers went about openly, continuing the work of Jesus.
They healed (Acts 3.1–10),
they preached (Acts 3.11–26),
and they baptised (Acts 2.40–42).

READ ACTS 2.43–47 TO FIND OUT HOW THOSE FIRST CHRISTIANS SPENT THEIR TIME.

But this happy group soon caused concern. The High Priest and the members of the Sadducee party did not like the group's popularity, and took every opportunity to find fault.

The Christians were hounded, thrown into jail, and ordered never again to speak in the name of Jesus.

One Pharisee, however, was cautious:

Leave them alone! If what they have planned and done is of human origin, it will disappear, but if it comes from God, you cannot possibly defeat them!

(Acts 5. 38–39, GNB)

The little Church, fearing for its safety, decided to scatter. Some of the Christians went to Samaria, to Gaza, and to places further away, taking with them the GOOD NEWS of Jesus Christ.

Everywhere they went they were in danger, and met secretly, often in each other's houses.

## THE CHRISTIAN CHURCH IN THE CATACOMBS

For nearly 300 years after Pentecost, people who followed Christ - the first CHRISTIANS - were hated and persecuted.

They were said to be traitors for refusing to worship the Roman Emperor.

When it was known that they had a custom of drinking wine and eating bread, calling them the blood and flesh of Christ, the Christians were labelled 'cannibals'!

So Christian men, women and children had to meet secretly. They became, literally, an 'underground movement.'

Deep under the outskirts of Rome there were caves and complex passages. These 'catacombs' as they were called, were where the Romans buried their dead, in niches in the cave walls.

Christian groups found the catacombs just right for their secret meetings, and here the Church of God grew in strength and size.

If caught, the Christians were punished. They were thrown to the lions, made to fight with gladiators, lit as human torches, or crucified.

THEN THINGS CHANGED

About the year 330 AD the Roman Emperor Constantine gave Christians their freedom, and became a Christian himself.

# THE CHURCH THROUGH THE AGES

CENTURY → 1st

**PENTECOST**

The power of the Holy Spirit is given to the first group of Christ's followers

The first Christians are Jews. They worship in existing synagogues.

Gentiles (non-Jews) are welcomed into Christianity.

Christians begin to break away from Jewish traditions. They worship on the first day of the week instead of the Sabbath. Easter and Pentecost are celebrated as Festivals.

CENTURY → 2nd – 4th

The message of Christ is spreading rapidly. Small groups of Christians are meeting, in secret, far and wide. They meet in caves, in tombs, and in small hidden villages. Somehow they must be held together, so leaders meet to put into words what Christians believe. These words are the creeds. Everywhere it is dangerous to be a Christian. Men, women and children are tortured and murdered for following Christ.

4th

The Roman Emperor, Constantine, dreams about the cross of Christ, and becomes a Christian. He orders Christianity to become the official religion of the Roman world.

Now Christians are FREE – to worship God openly, and to build their own churches. But.....

4th

. . . freedom often leads to laziness and arguments. Church bishops want to keep an unbroken line from the first apostles, through themselves, to all bishops in the future.

The writings of the New Testament are gathered together.

11th

Rome is now the centre for the Church in the West. *Il Papa* — a Pope — is appointed as leader of the western Church.

The State is becoming controlled by the Church.

Constantinople is the centre for the Church in the East. A Patriarch is appointed the eastern Church leader.

The Church in the East is controlled by the State.

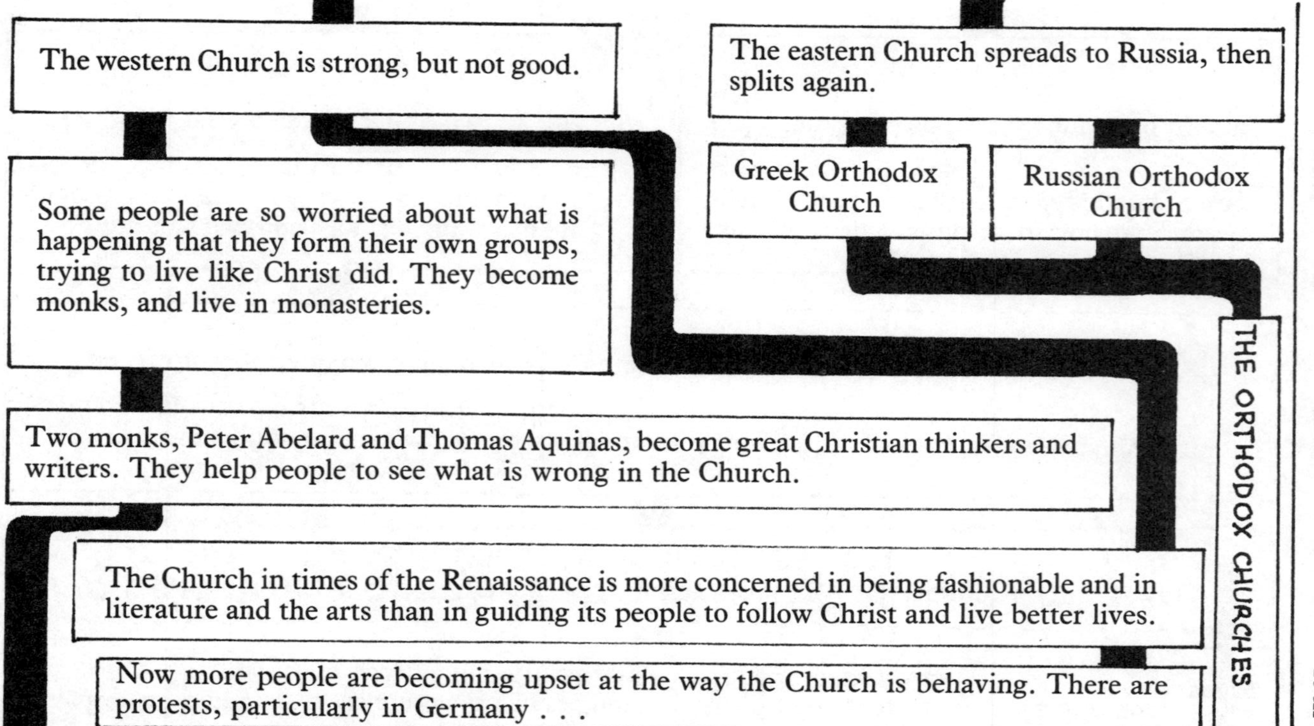
10th — 13th
12th — 13th
15th
The western Church is strong, but not good.
The eastern Church spreads to Russia, then splits again.
Greek Orthodox Church
Russian Orthodox Church
THE ORTHODOX CHURCHES
Some people are so worried about what is happening that they form their own groups, trying to live like Christ did. They become monks, and live in monasteries.
Two monks, Peter Abelard and Thomas Aquinas, become great Christian thinkers and writers. They help people to see what is wrong in the Church.
The Church in times of the Renaissance is more concerned in being fashionable and in literature and the arts than in guiding its people to follow Christ and live better lives.
Now more people are becoming upset at the way the Church is behaving. There are protests, particularly in Germany . . .

THE ORTHODOX CHURCHES GO ON

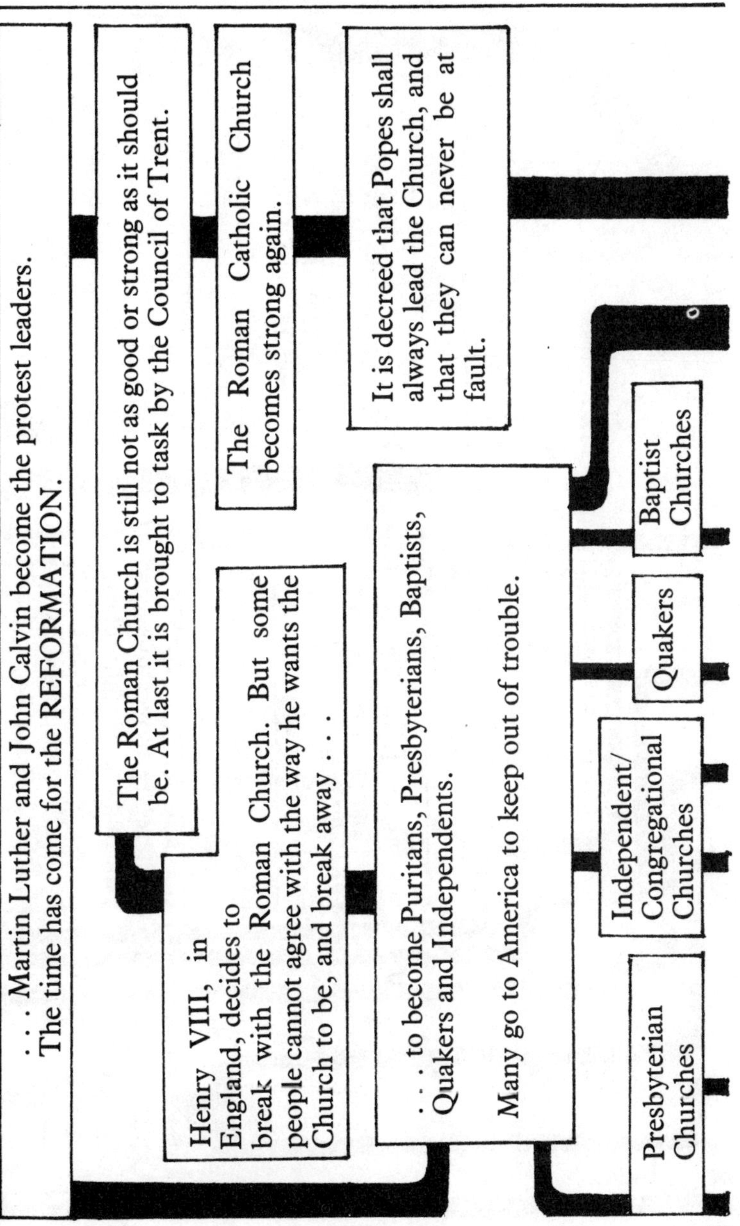

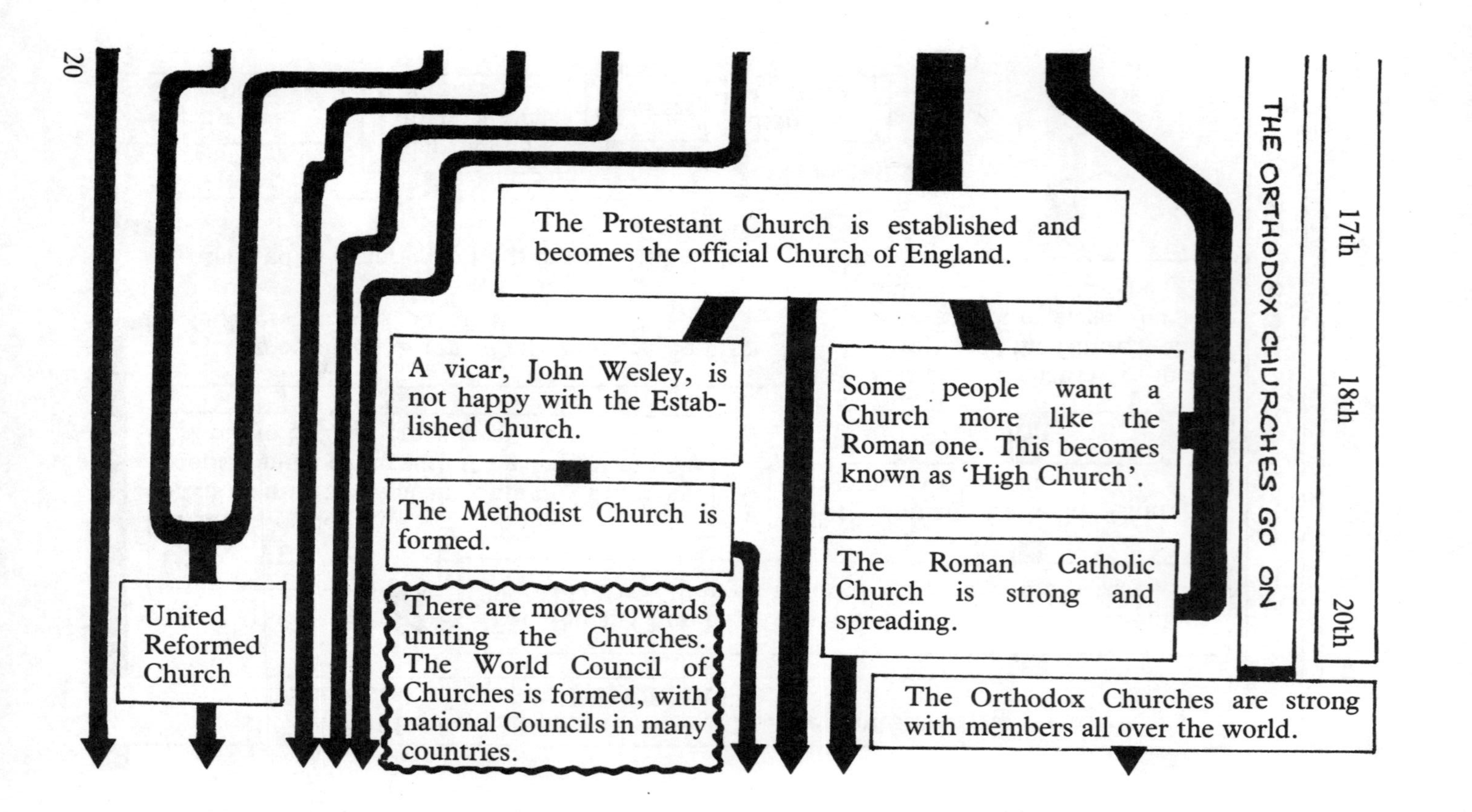
17th
18th
20th
THE ORTHODOX CHURCHES GO ON
The Protestant Church is established and becomes the official Church of England.
Some people want a Church more like the Roman one. This becomes known as 'High Church'.
The Roman Catholic Church is strong and spreading.
The Orthodox Churches are strong with members all over the world.
A vicar, John Wesley, is not happy with the Established Church.
The Methodist Church is formed.
There are moves towards uniting the Churches. The World Council of Churches is formed, with national Councils in many countries.
United Reformed Church

# MONASTERIES AND MONKS

About 250 years after the first Christians formed their small secret groups, the Christian religion became 'fashionable'. The Church was strong, but not always Christ-like, and individuals began to leave the organised churches to follow Christ's way of life on their own. These men – and a few women – lived lives of extreme simplicity in caves, as hermits. Some even made their lives harder by spending years sitting on top of pillars!

So these people, beginning with those who lived in caves in the Egyptian deserts, got together in groups and built the first MONASTERIES

(In Greek, the word for ALONE was MONOS)

Soon, communities of religious men had sprung up all round the Mediterranean Sea, and there were even some in Britain. Christianity had spread to our shores when Britain was under Roman rule.

In the 5th Century Britain was invaded by heathens who drove the monks west to Wales and Cornwall, and to the North-West of Scotland.

Look in an atlas to see how many places in these areas have LLAN or CAPEL in their names. These were where the first wooden chapels (CAPELS) with green lawns (LLANS) were established. Can you find Llandrindod Wells and Capel Curig?

SAINT PATRICK

I took Christianity to Ireland from the west of Britain

SAINT COLUMBA

Later I went from Ireland to take the faith to Scotland

## IN SCOTLAND

-on the small Island of Iona, Columba founded a monastery. Look for this island on a map: it is just off the Island of Mull.

## IN THE NORTH OF ENGLAND

-monasteries were built, but the people in the south were mostly non-Christians.

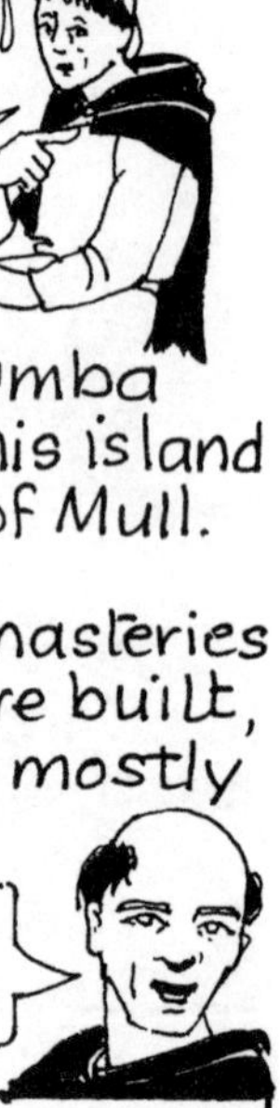

—until I, Augustine, was sent from Rome to convert England!

Augustine did such good work that he was made the first Archbishop of Canterbury. King Ethelbert himself became a Christian just before Columba died on Iona.

Benedict made a set of rules for his monks:

Monks who followed Benedict's rules spread far and wide, setting up houses of religious men. They became known as Benedictine monks, and wore black robes. Sometimes they were called Black Monks or Black Friars. There was once a settlement at Blackfriars, in London. The Benedictines became famous for their learning and art.

Monks in other monasteries followed similar rules, and became known as Dominicans, Jesuits, Franciscans, and Carmelites. There are monks and nuns today who still live according to the RULES made hundreds of years ago.

Some of the buildings in which the monks lived were built by themselves. Most people thought monasteries were important, so money was given freely. Eventually special architects and craftsmen were employed to erect great churches for monks to worship in. Many of the religious houses were known as ABBEYS or PRIORIES.

By this time there were also NUNNERIES, or CONVENTS, for women who wanted to serve God together.

In a Monastery or Abbey, there were usually several important positions:

The ABBOT or PRIOR was chosen by the monks to lead them. He had to be good and wise because he was their 'father.' As the community grew, and became wealthier, the Abbot became more important. Often he had one - or two - 'deputies'.

Monks, also, had special positions and duties:

- and the Chamberlain looked after the bedding, the Hospitaller welcomed guests, and the Master of Novices was in charge of young men and boys.

A MEDIEVAL MONASTERY
Barns, stables, brewery
Cornfields
Orchard
Bees
Vegetable garden
Guest House
Lay brothers' Infirmary
Lay brothers' dormitory and refectory
Mill
Cloisters
Monks' refectory
Chapter House
CHURCH
Cemetery for monks
Monks' dormitory
Kitchen
Infirmary
Chapel
Gardens
Stream
Pasture land
Abbot's lodging
CHAPTER HOUSE - Monks' private meeting place. REFECTORY - Dining room. DORMITORY - Sleeping quarters. INFIRMARY - Hospital. CLOISTERS - open walk for prayer and meditation.

Over the years the monasteries became bigger, richer, and more important. The monks in them still felt they were part of the Roman Catholic Church.

Then, in the 16th Century, King Henry VIII of England wanted to divorce his wife. He asked the Pope for permission, but the Pope refused.

I am FURIOUS! All Roman Catholics are out of favour!

So King Henry VIII planned to ruin the monasteries...

They are full of valuable treasures, Sire. Why not pass a law saying they all belong to YOU now?

Good idea, chief minister. I will dissolve all the monasteries!

**Act of Dissolution**

Nine thousand monks, canons and nuns are to be dismissed.

All valuables will go to the crown.

Henry VIII, 1536

Some monasteries survived, however, and are still strong today. Many of them can be visited. Try to see those at Aylesford in Kent; Farnborough in Hampshire, or Mount St Bernard, near Loughborough in Leicestershire.

## FINDING OUT ABOUT THE CHURCH

Not all churches are organised in the same way. There are many different *denominations* of churches, which go back hundreds of years. Gradually the denominations have developed different ways of leadership and organisation.

There is the *Roman Catholic Church*, which is led and governed from Rome in Italy, and whose overall leader is the Pope.

There is the *Church of England*, which is Protestant and is often called the Anglican Church.

There are also many other Protestant Churches which are called *Nonconformist* or *Free Churches*. For example, Methodist, Baptist, and United Reformed Churches are nonconformist.

*Discover all you can about your own church. If you compare your answers to the questions with someone who goes to a church of a different denomination, you will probably find many ways in which your churches are alike, and some in which they differ.*

*There is a lot to find out in the section that follows. Do not try to do it all at once. Most of the answers can be found by asking questions of the leaders and members of your church, and by looking at notice-boards and reading the church magazine or news-letter.*

# THE WORK OF THE CHURCH

Worship, caring for each other, and serving other people, are important parts of the work of the church. Doing these things involves everyone who belongs to the church.

But churches appoint some people to do special jobs.

Minister, Vicar or Priest?

Most churches have someone who leads worship, helps people in the church, and encourages them to show God's love in the world. Such a person is called a *minister, pastor, rector, vicar* or *priest.*

Like the teachers in a school, ministers and priests must be fully trained for the job. They believe that God has called them to do this work.

At a theological college they learn about the Bible and the Christian faith. They learn how to conduct services, how to help people with problems, and how to encourage people to live as Christians.

Some ministers and vicars take on a wider responsibility in the Church. They may be *Bishops, District Chairmen, Provincial Moderators* or *Area Superintendents.*

Find out how your minister or vicar trained:
the qualifications needed,
the subjects studied,
the practical work done.

Find out:
How your church would set about getting a new vicar or minister if your present one left.

When your minister or vicar goes on holiday, does your church close down?
If not, someone else must lead the services; how is that person chosen and invited?
Whose job is it to welcome and look after the invited leader?

## IMPORTANT JOBS

Many other people in the church work with the minister or vicar.

Some serve the church by becoming *elders*, *deacons*, or *members of a church council*.

Find out how the church appoints them and what they do.

Sometimes people who are not ministers preach in their own or other churches. These men and women are called *lay preachers*. They are usually given some training.

Are there any lay preachers in your church?
Ask them how they train, and if they are required to pass any examinations.
Are they paid to do this job?
Do they do it full-time or part-time?

Many churches have people who take on special duties to help run the church.

In your church, who cleans or takes care of the church buildings?
Is he or she called a *caretaker*, or is there another title for this job?
Try to interview this person to discover what his or her special duties are.

Find out:

Has your church a *secretary*?
How does he or she help the church?
What does a *treasurer* do in a church?
How is the money given by the congregation each week used?

If your church building needed to be repaired or redecorated:

Who would be responsible for seeing that the work was done?
How would it be paid for?

Sometimes decisions need to be made which concern the people who worship in the church.

Perhaps the hymnbooks are old and need replacing; who decides whether new, modern ones, or simply new books of the same kind, are chosen?
Perhaps someone from the church should attend a conference, meeting or other function; who is to be appointed?

Who makes decisions such as these in your church? Is there a meeting of all the members, or are decisions left to a council or committee?

# OTHER LOCAL CHURCHES

Find out if there is a Council of Churches in your town, and make a list of all the denominations represented on it.

Does your church link up with other churches for special occasions or services?

Do the ministers, pastors and vicars meet together regularly?

Do you know how other churches, of different denominations, are governed and organised?

*Find out about the ways in which churches are the same, and ways in which they are different.*

# STRANGE – BUT TRUE!

A church in Grasmere, Cumbria, holds a Rush Bearing Festival in August each year. Men and women, boys and girls, carrying rushes and flowers, walk all round the village. The church, to which the procession returns, is also strewn with rushes.

In the churchyard in Wood Plumpton, Lancashire, a 'witch' - Meg - is buried. A large boulder was placed on top of her grave – to stop her getting out!

Outside St Martin's church, in Guernsey, there is a statue of 'La Gran'mère du Chimquière' which is about 4,000 years old. The church, like many others, was built on the site of pagan worship, and the old pagan statues were 'consecrated', making them acceptable to Christians. Sometimes brides being married at the church hang garlands of flowers round La Gran'mere's neck.

St Petroch's church is believed to be the last church in Devon where the singing was regularly accompanied by a band of 'minstrels' or musicians. There is still a minstrels' gallery in the church.

# BUILDINGS FOR WORSHIP

THE CHURCH OF GOD is not a building: it is PEOPLE. Christians, whether they live in Britain or Burma, Botswana or Bolivia, make up this Church.

It is confusing that the buildings in which Christians worship God are also called churches.

Sometimes these churches are called chapels, or cathedrals, meeting-houses or citadels.

They have all been designed, however differently, as places where Christians can meet together to express their faith in God.

Some are large, some small. Some are dark and silent, others are bright and airy. There are plain, simple churches; there are richly decorated ones.

## LET'S LOOK AT CATHEDRALS.......

Cathedrals are just very large churches. Each one is the 'home' of a Bishop.

During the middle ages cathedrals were built all over Europe. Each set of builders tried to make its building bigger and better than all the rest.

Many cathedrals were built on the highest hill in a town where they could dominate the smaller houses and market stalls.

A great number of these enormous churches had pinnacles and pointed arches, leading peoples' eyes upward.

Inside, beautifully decorated stained-glass windows told stories from the Bible for the people who could not read.

Cathedrals in medieval days were rich in decoration and ornaments, in sculptures and carvings.

It cost a lot of money to design and build a cathedral, and it took many years to complete it. In medieval times bishops had to raise the money needed, and did not always go about this in good, honest ways.

The bishop employed a master-mason to organise the work.

The master-mason drew up his plan for the building, then called in his workmen.

Travelling craftsmen, also called masons, were employed. The masons who did the heavy work, like erecting the stone walls and pillars, were called the **SETTLERS** or **WALLERS**.

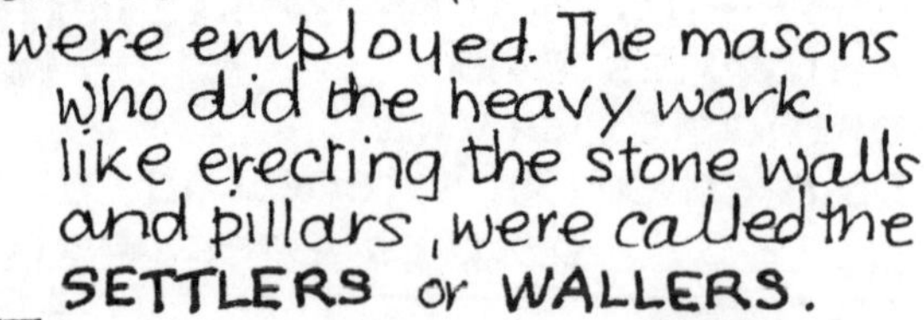

**FREE MASONS** were employed to do the carving and decorative work.

These masons first made their own **LODGE** in which to live. The designs and patterns were traced in the Lodge, and templates made.

Local peasants were used for any unskilled work.

## LOOK INSIDE A CATHEDRAL

Here is the **PLAN** of a cathedral. Another cathedral would have a different plan, because no two are exactly alike. But most cathedrals, especially old ones, have things in common – a nave, and altars, for instance.

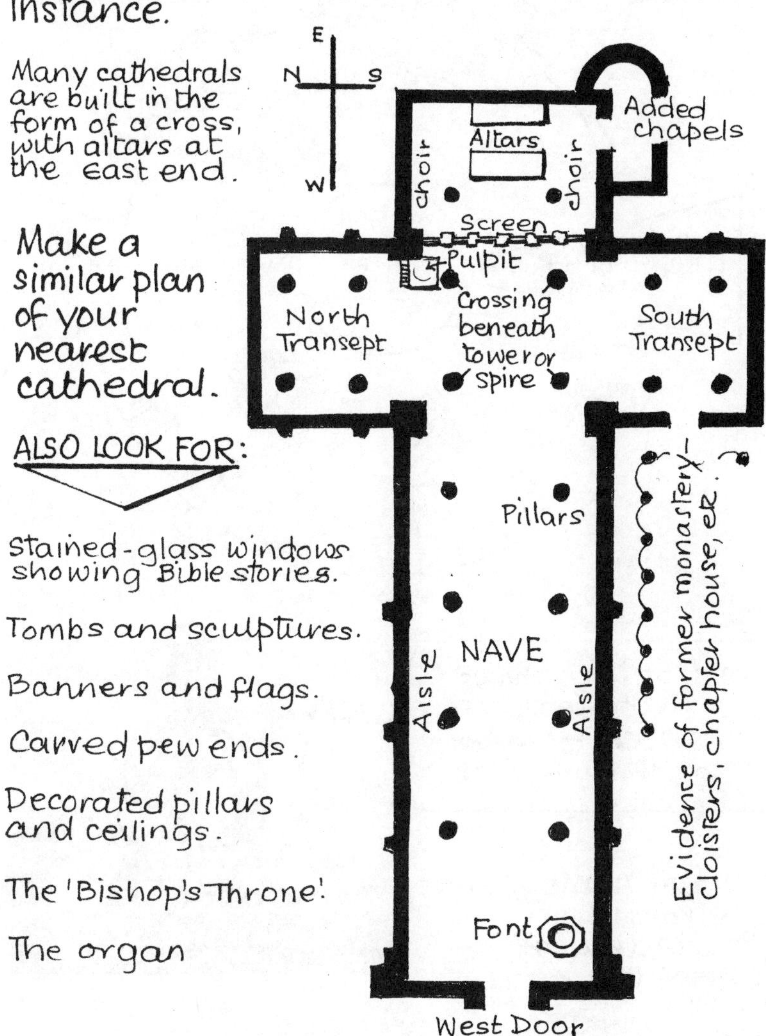


Many cathedrals are built in the form of a cross, with altars at the east end.

Make a similar plan of your nearest cathedral.

ALSO LOOK FOR:

Stained-glass windows showing Bible stories.

Tombs and sculptures.

Banners and flags.

Carved pew ends.

Decorated pillars and ceilings.

The 'Bishop's Throne'.

The organ

**COMPARE** the plan of an old cathedral with the modern one, below, which was built at Liverpool and consecrated in 1967.

WHAT DIFFERENCES CAN YOU SEE?

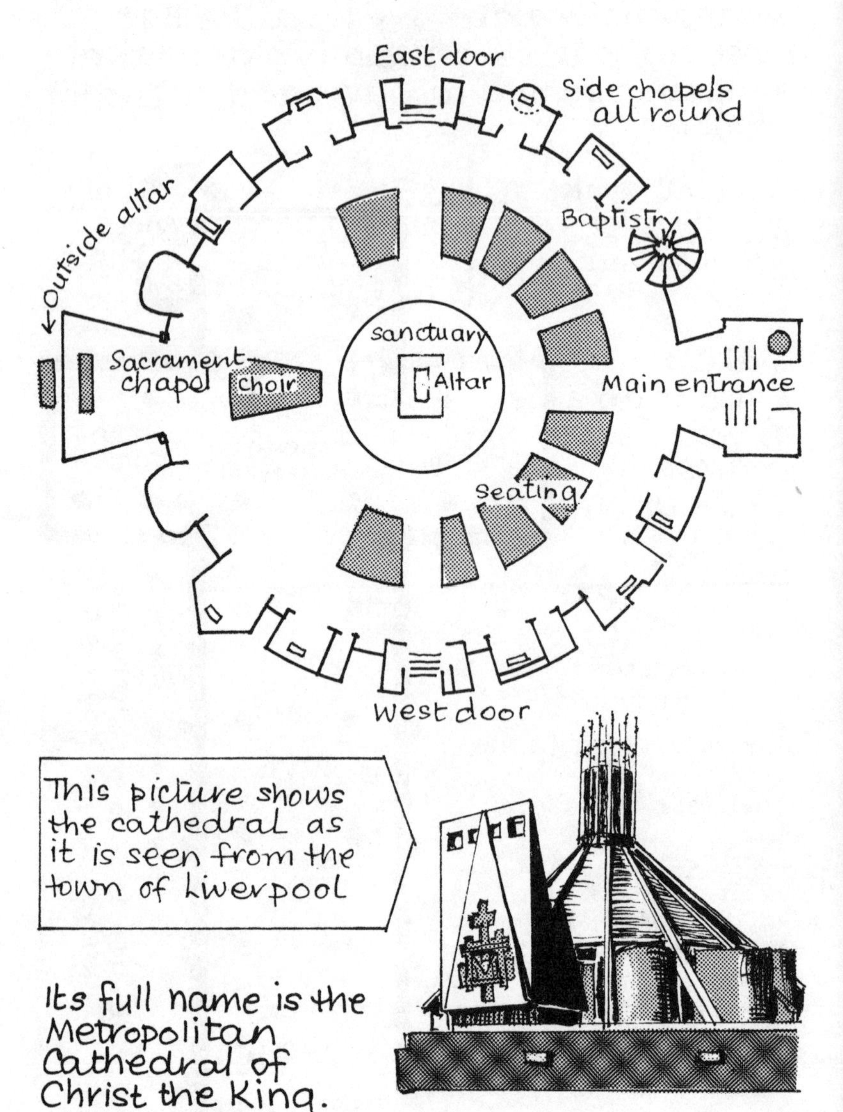


This picture shows the cathedral as it is seen from the town of Liverpool

Its full name is the Metropolitan Cathedral of Christ the King.

# LET'S LOOK AT OTHER CHURCHES

In some places of worship - eg. the Baptist, United Reformed, and Methodist churches, there is usually no altar. The pulpit, from which the minister or leader speaks to the people, is often the focal point, and there is a table for communion services.

People attending these churches want to feel that they ARE the Church, a fellowship of people meeting to worship God together, each person being equal in the sight of God.

This plan, of a United Reformed Church, gives an idea of what a NON-CONFORMIST church may be like. Find out what a Baptist Church or chapel has that is not found in other non-conformist churches.

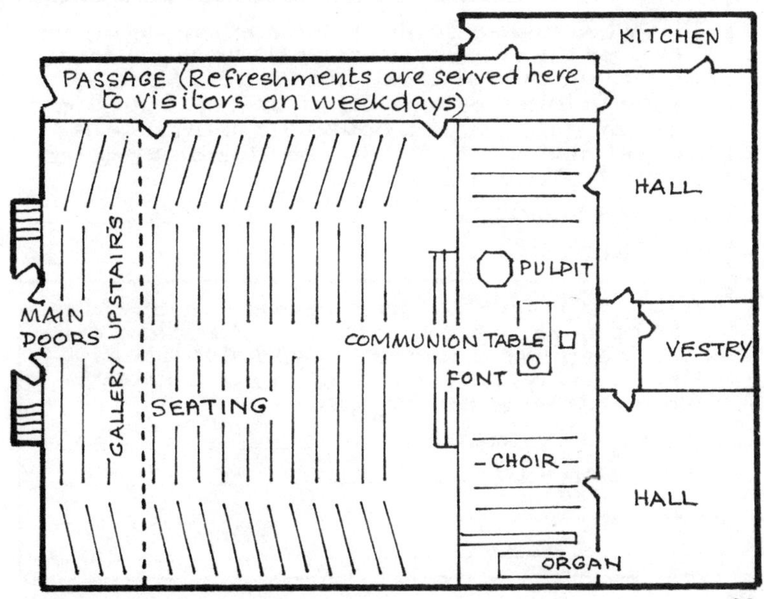

# THINGS TO LOOK FOR–
## OUTSIDE A CHURCH

Look for all these things. Make a note of where you see them. Trace and colour the pictures, or draw your own.

**1 STONE CROSS.** Before the Reformation people often listened to the preacher here. The priest could point to the cross and tell everyone about the life and death of Jesus Christ.

Seen at: ______________________

**2 TOMBSTONES.** Read what is written on them; you will learn a lot about families who worshipped in the church long ago. Important or rich people had very large tombs. Make a note of any epitaphs in rhyme, or amusing ones.

Seen at: ______________________

**3 LYCH GATE.** 'Lych' was the Saxon word for CORPSE. At this place the body was transferred from a cart or wagon to the wheeled 'bier', before being taken into the church. Sometimes there are wall benches or seats in the lych gate.

Seen at: ______________________

**4 TOWER and/or SPIRE.** Is the one you see in the centre of the church, or at the West end, or does it stand alone? The tower used to be a place of refuge in times of war, flood, or fire. Does the tower or spire you see house the church bells? Can you also see a lightning conductor showing on the highest point?

Tower seen at: ______________________

Spire seen at: ______________________

**5 WEATHER VANE.** This is usually on top of the tower or spire, and shows wind direction. Often it is shaped like a cockerel. Read Matthew 26.69-75 to find out why. Look for, and make a note of, other weather vane shapes.

Cockerel seen at: ______________________

Other shapes seen: ______________________

______________________

______________________

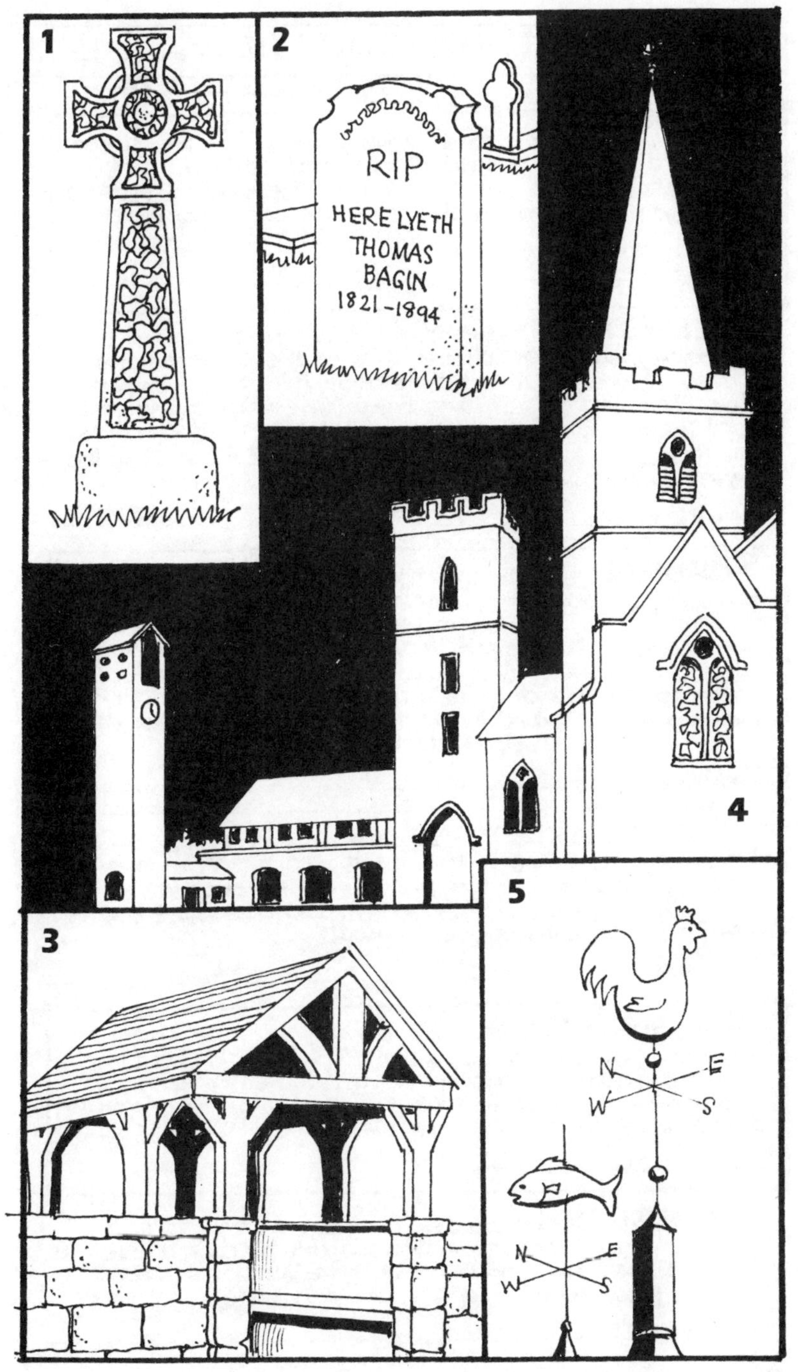
1
2
RIP
HERE LYETH
THOMAS
BAGIN
1821-1894
4
3
5
N
E
W
S
N
E
W
S

## MORE THINGS TO LOOK FOR......

**6 SCRATCH DIAL.** Sometimes carved in the South wall, this was a kind of sundial, with a rod in the centre whose shadow fell on the straight lines. This told people when the service was about to begin.

Seen at: ____________________

**7 YEW TREES.** These were often planted in graveyards. Because they were evergreens they were said to represent life going on and on. The branches are sometimes used instead of palms on Palm Sunday. Bows and arrows used to be made of yew wood. The berries of the yew are poisonous to animals.

Seen at: ____________________

**8 CHURCH DOOR or PORCH.** Some entrances have large porches, which were used as meeting places or school rooms for the village people. Look for seats in the porch. Above the door you may see a figure of Christ, who said 'I am the door.' (John 10.9) The door is usually heavy, and may have a sanctuary knocker. Find out what this is for and when it would have been used.

Seen at: ____________________

**9 GARGOYLE.** These are really water-spouts, taking rain from the roof away from the church walls. Gargoyles are often carved into monsters or grotesque animal shapes, probably to frighten evil spirits away!

Seen at: ____________________

**10 MASON'S MARKS.** You may see strange marks cut into the wall of the church. Each builder-mason had his 'signature' or sign to show he had helped erect the church. Other such signs were made by pilgrims as they travelled round.

Seen at: ____________________

**11 CHAINS.** If you see a chain attached to a church wall, or signs of a chain-holder, these were put up for farmers to tie their cattle to before entering the church.

Seen at ____________________

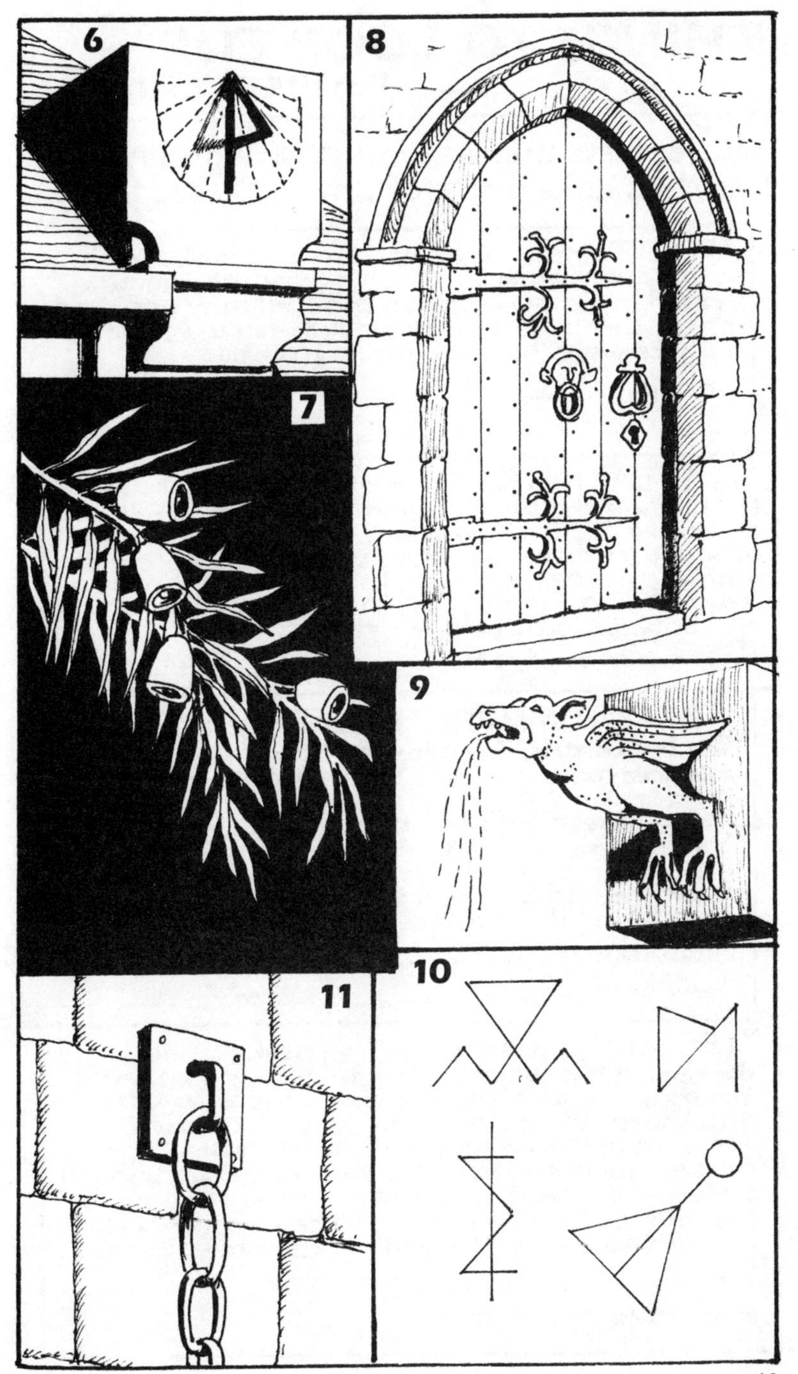
6
7
8
9
10
11

# THINGS TO LOOK FOR– INSIDE A CHURCH

Look for these things in your church and in other churches. Make a note of where you see them.

**1** PULPIT. The word 'pulpit' means a platform, so it is usually raised. This is where the minister preaches the sermon, so that all may see and hear. Until the end of the 14th century, all pulpits were OUTSIDE the churches!

Seen at ______________________

and ______________________

**2** FONT/BAPTISTRY. The font is a bowl or basin for holding the water used in Baptism. Often the structure holding the basin is large and ornate, of wood or stone. In some churches the font is small, and can be moved. In others, there is a 'baptistry', a large 'pool' in which people coming for Baptism can be immersed.

What is used in your church? ______________________

**3** ALTAR/COMMUNION TABLE. The altar, where the bread and wine for the Holy Communion Service are placed, is sometimes almost hidden by a 'rood screen'. Look for altar rails, where people kneel to take Communion. Some churches have a 'Communion table' instead of an altar, reminding people of the table round which Jesus and his disciples sat during their last supper together.

Altar seen at ______________________

Table seen at ______________________

**4** LECTERN. This is a reading desk to hold the open Bible. Usually made of wood or brass, you may see one shaped like an eagle with outspread wings. The eagle is used because it is a bird that flies and nests in the highest places, and symbolises the Word of God being winged across the world. In some churches you can see evidence of rings and chains where the Bible used to be protected from thieves.

The shape I saw was ______________________

In my church the lectern is ______________________

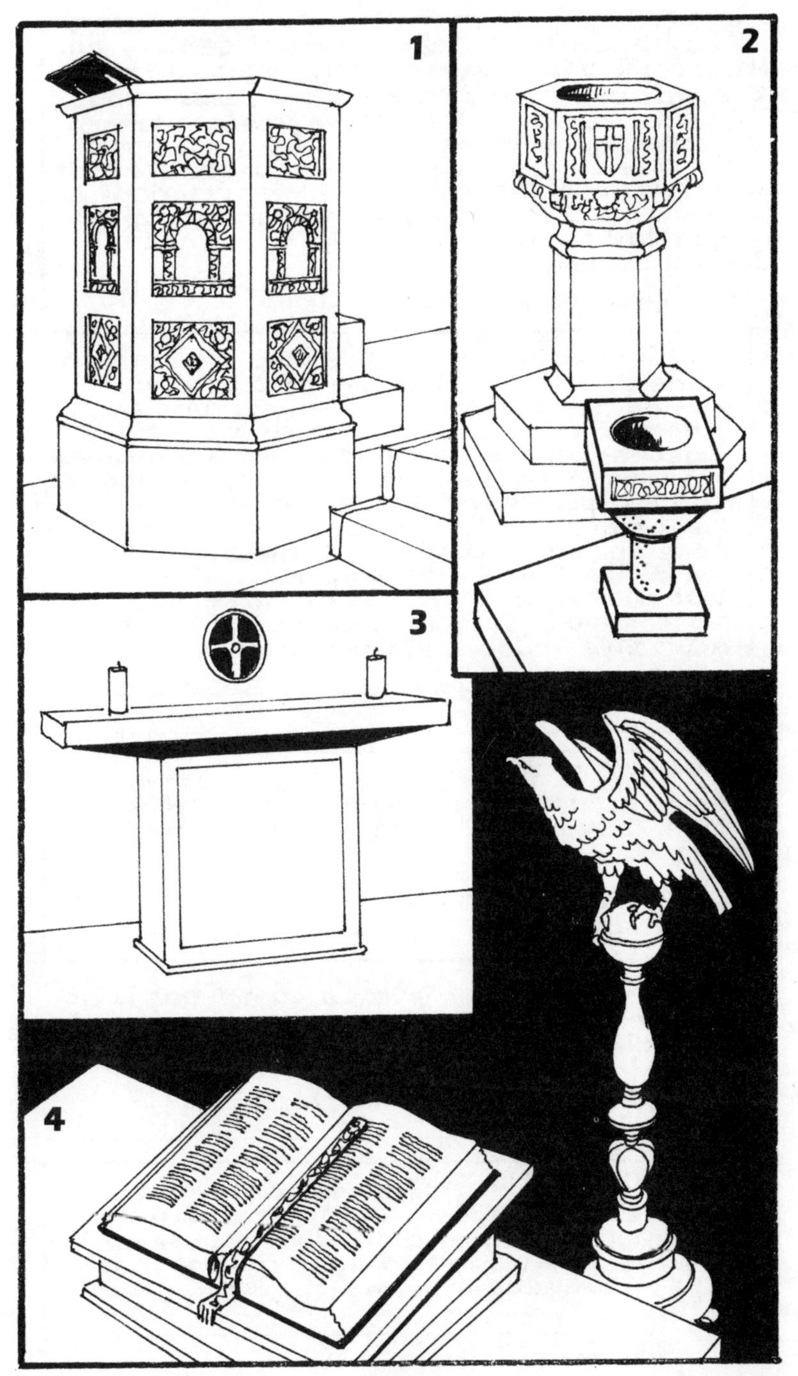
1
2
3
4

**5** PEWS/CHAIRS. Before the 15th century all the people stood during church services; only the sick or old went to the stone seats round the walls. You can still see these seats in some churches today. In the 17th century many pews were boxed in, and furnished with padded seats and hat pegs. These were for the very rich. Many churches now have chairs instead of pews, which can be moved easily to suit what is taking place.

Our church has pews ☐, or chairs ☐. (Tick)

**6** WINDOWS. In the middle ages craftsmen made the church windows colourful with stained glass, cutting and arranging small pieces of coloured glass which were held together with strips of lead. These windows showed pictures of biblical events, and saints, and told people the stories they could not read for themselves. Later, many windows like this were destroyed, as they were thought to be too distracting for worship. Now, people think that making a church beautiful really helps the worship of God. You may find some very attractive modern stained glass windows.

The window I saw showed: ____________________

____________________

**7** CORBELS. These are carvings made in wood or stone, usually at the meeting of a beam and a wall. They are often shaped like angels or demons.

Seen at: ____________________

Shaped like: ____________________

**8** BOSSES. A boss is like a corbel, but is at the meeting point of the 'ribs' of a decorated ceiling. Bosses often show shields or small intricate carvings, but are usually too high to be seen properly!

Bosses seen at: ____________________

**9** POPPY HEAD. This is the name given to the carved tops of pew-ends. Generally they are trefoil shaped and are often made up of carved leaves, but you may find some in the shape of animals or human figures.

Seen at: ____________________

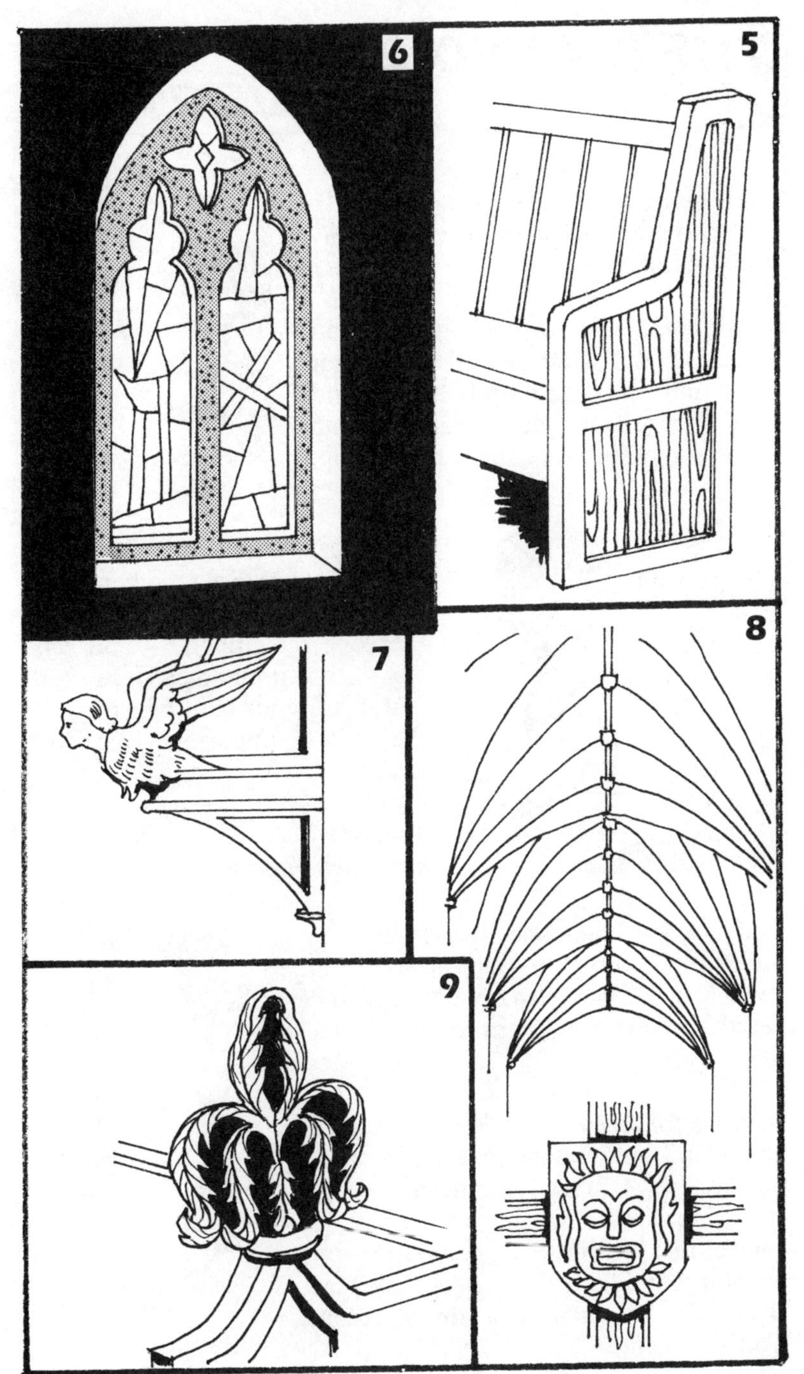
6
5
7
8
9

# THE INGREDIENTS OF WORSHIP

When you say, about a pop-singer, 'He (or she) is really great!' you are, in a way, worshipping him or her.

Worshipping God means saying, 'God, you are great!' God is our maker, our ruler, our Saviour, and our friend. Worshipping Someone so great is natural — it is something we cannot help doing.

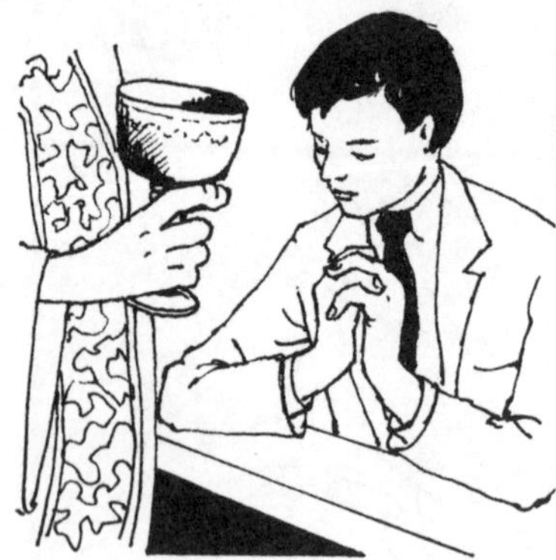

For most Christians, the *Holy Communion Service*, where the bread and wine are shared, where everyone remembers — and acts out — the simple meal Jesus had with his friends before he died, is the most important part of worship.

*You can find out more about this meal from pages 57-58.*

God is great, fantastic, wonderful, yes; but, unlike the pop-singer, he is near enough to be spoken to quietly, and to be heard if we listen with our minds. We call this *prayer*.

In some churches people kneel to pray, as one would bow before royalty; in others people simply bow their heads as they speak to God, closing their eyes to concentrate on his presence. And some worshippers lift their arms as they pray, showing how open they are to receive God's blessing.

When we are happy, it is natural to sing. *Hymns and songs* have been part of worship since the very earliest days of the Church. Jesus and his disciples sang hymns to God — read Mark 14.26.

When you are singing hymns, decide, by studying the words, whether they are praising hymns or prayer hymns. Are they saying, 'How wonderful God is!' or 'Lord, I need help, or guidance, or to give you thanks'?

In the church service, *the Bible* holds a special place, not only by its position (does your church keep a large Bible in a certain place?) but by the fact that parts of it are read to the whole congregation week by week. People may follow these readings in their own Bibles, or in ones provided by the church, or they may prefer to sit back and just listen to God's word being read.

In most churches there will be a leader — a priest or minister — who is specially trained to lead the worship. Usually this person will deliver a *sermon* to the people: a talk to help them understand God's word, to encourage their faith, and to guide them as they try to live as Christians in the community.

Some churches use a *liturgy* for their services. This is a set form of words, prayers and readings, fixed for each Sunday in the year, and is used by the priest and the congregation.

In other churches there is no set form of worship. There may be long periods of silence — for meditation — or loud, spontaneous cries of praise, and handclapping.

People are different. Church services vary, too. Some are full of ritual and solemnity, others are informal and simple. But Christians all over the world, in whatever form of service, are saying the same thing as they worship:

**GOD, YOU ARE GREAT!**

# WORSHIP IN YOUR CHURCH

Watch as people enter the church: do they say a silent prayer? Is the church quiet, or is there a friendly hum of conversation? Is the Bible carried into the church, or is it already there?

What happens next? Do the people stand as the priest or minister enters? Does he 'call the people to worship' with a few words from the Bible or a sentence of welcome?

Do you use a set prayer book, or do you follow the words of the prayers said by the church leader? Are people in the congregation encouraged to pray aloud? Is the Lord's Prayer said, or sung, every week? Do most people sit to pray, or kneel, or stand?

For the hymns, is there an organ, or piano, or other instruments to accompany the singing? What hymn-book(s) are used? Can you find out what hymn-books are used in other local churches? Do you often learn new hymns or songs? Do the children sing on their own at any time?

What version of the Bible is used for the Bible readings? Do the people have copies so that they can follow the readings themselves? How many Bible readings are there in the service? Who usually reads them out loud: the minister, or someone from the congregation?

Is there an offertory? Find out what the money is used for. Do some people put little envelopes containing money into the plate or bag? Find out why.

What happens at the end of the service? Is there a *Benediction*? Do people say the *Peace* together? Where does the minister stand when the people leave the church? Are any refreshments served so that people can meet together after the service?

# THE SACRAMENTS

**What is a Sacrament?**

There is an invisible bond of love which exists between parents and children. It is quite surprising that, even when they are neglected or ill-treated, most children continue to love their parents. And however naughty or difficult children might be, they are almost always deeply loved by their parents.

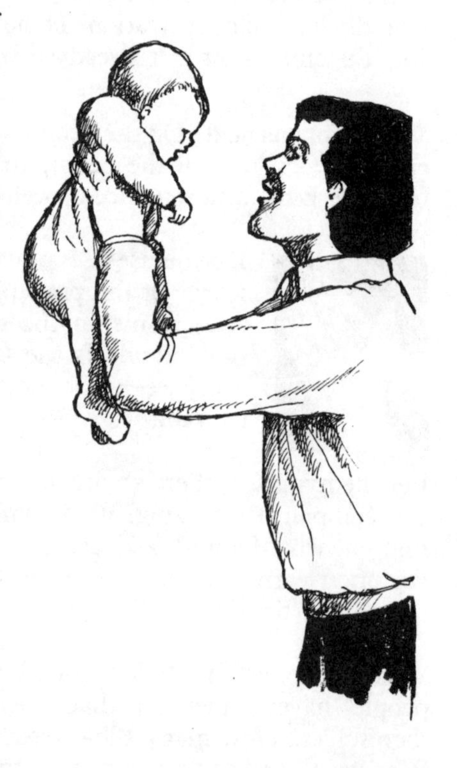

This love is *felt* but it is invisible. Parents and children can also *show* their love: they can cuddle and kiss; they can care for each other in a physical way that is seen.

Just as parents love their children, so God loves us and we love him.

It is an invisible love, a *felt* love; but there are also outward signs that *show* that love. These are called sacraments.

The number of sacraments varies in different types or denominations of churches. In the Roman Catholic Church there are seven, including Baptism, Confirmation, Confession, the Eucharist, and Matrimony. The Anglican Church has a number of these sacraments, but most nonconformist churches, such as the Baptist, the Methodist and the United Reformed Churches, have only two — Baptism and Holy Communion.

## BAPTISM

The New Testament tells about John the Baptist (Mark 1.4-8), but baptism was not a new thing at that time. For years, Jews had baptised people who were converted to Judaism.

John the Baptist declared that people should prepare themselves, by 'washing away their sins', for the coming of a new and better way of life, for the Kingdom of God. John probably knew the words of the prophet Ezekiel:

> 'I will sprinkle clean water on you and make you clean . . . I will give you a new heart and a new mind.'
>
> (Ezekiel 36.25-26, GNB)

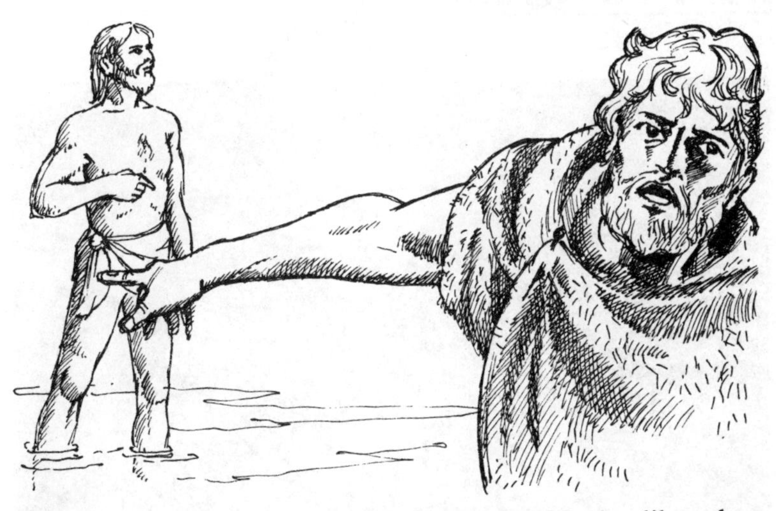

When Jesus was baptised by John, the Spirit of God — like a dove — came upon him. Later, when Jesus was instructing his disciples to carry on his work after he had left them, he said: 'Go, then, to all peoples everywhere and make them my disciples: baptise them in the name of the Father, the Son, and the Holy Spirit.'

(Matthew 28.19, GNB)

Baptism became an important part of the early Church's work and witness. It was believed that those who were baptised were forgiven by God for their sins, that Christ gave them the power to lead new lives, and that, by baptism, they were received into the Church.

Perhaps it was because at first whole families were baptised that it became the custom, in many churches, to baptise very young children.

But a small baby cannot be said to 'believe', or to make a decision about his or her faith, so parents, and sometimes godparents, are asked at the baby's baptism to promise to give the child every opportunity and encouragement to grow up as a Christian, so that he or she, when old enough, will confirm the promise by being *confirmed* or received into membership of the Church.

## CONFIRMATION

Baptist Churches believe that baptism should be only for those who are able to make their own promises and affirmations of faith: they must understand what is meant by baptism. The person who comes for baptism is usually completely immersed in water, as Jesus was in the River Jordan.

If you attend a Baptist church, you will know where the baptistry is; that is, the tank which holds the water used in a baptismal service. If you belong to another church, try to find a Baptist friend who will take you to a Baptist church. You might show that Baptist friend the font that is used in your church during infant baptism.

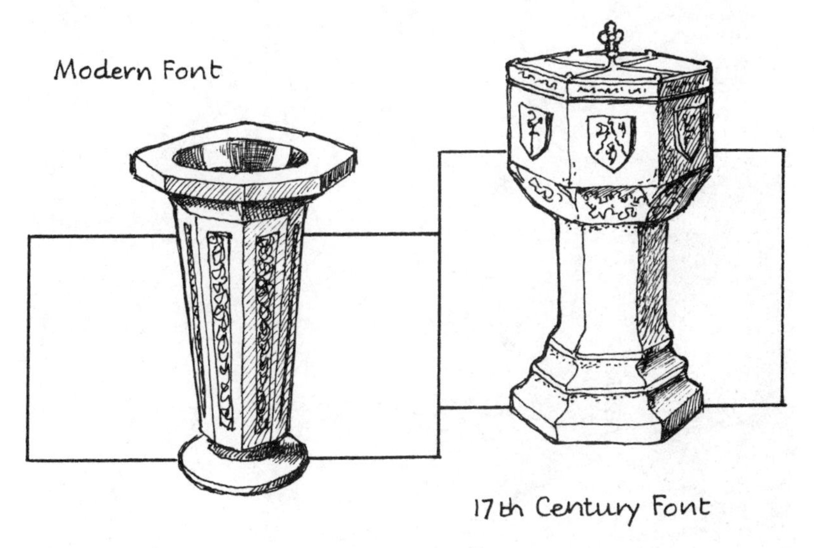


During infant baptism, the baby is brought to the font by his or her parents.

In Anglican churches this is sometimes done during a special service held in the afternoon, rather than in the morning. Several families may come to have their children baptised at the same time.

In nonconformist churches the baby is usually baptised at a time when the whole congregation is present, so that everybody in the church, and not only those in the immediate family, can join together in welcoming the baby into the church.

At the font the minister or vicar sprinkles the child's head with water, and makes the sign of a cross on its forehead. At the same time the priest will give the child the names that have been chosen by the parents.

In Baptist Churches, babies are brought to be *dedicated* by the minister, and to be given their names.

# HOLY COMMUNION

This is another of the sacraments of the Church.

'This is my body,' Jesus said as he broke the bread and handed it round to his disciples at their last supper together. And 'This is my blood poured out for many,' he said as he asked them to share a cup of wine.

The sacrament is known by a number of names. Roman Catholics usually call it the *Mass.* Other Christians use the name *Eucharist* (which comes from the Greek word meaning *thanksgiving*), *Holy Communion, The Lord's Supper* or *The Breaking of Bread.*

At the sacrament, Christians give thanks as they remember how Jesus died for them and for all people. Some believe that Christ is actually present with them.

Bread and wine are shared in different ways. Usually in Anglican and Methodist churches the people go to the rail in front of the altar or holy table to receive the *elements*. In other nonconformist churches the bread and wine are usually passed round to the people in their pews or seats. The leader of worship reads the words from the Bible which recall the last supper which Jesus shared with his friends.

The bread used in a Communion service varies from church to church. Sometimes small round wafers (a) are offered, specially baked without yeast. In other churches pieces of bread are broken off a large loaf (b), and in others slices of bread are cut into small cubes (c).

The cup or chalice which holds the wine is a symbol of the sacrament; so too is the dish or paten on which the bread is placed.

Look out for these symbols in churches you visit.

Most Christians say that the service of Holy Communion means more to them, and is more important, than any other service of the church. But it does not always have to take place in a church. Priests and ministers can give people the sacrament of Holy Communion in their own homes, in hospitals, and even in prisons.

The bread and the wine, and the words said at the service, are like the cuddle of a parent or the kiss of a child, which show their care and affection. They are the outward signs of an invisible love!

# THE BIBLE

The Bible is the sacred book of all Christians.

Other religions also have their sacred books.

All of these sacred books contain prayers, holy laws, poems, teachings and, in some of them, history. Like our Bible, many parts of these books were taught by 'word of mouth' before being written down. The stories and sayings in them were told from parent to child, and from the children to their children, until eventually they were written down for everyone to read.

The word *Bible* comes from the Greek word *biblia*, which means *books*. Our Bible contains many books, put together in one book.

The books that make up our Old Testament tell the story of a wandering people, who later became the people of Israel, the Jews. About 600 years before Jesus was born, when the Jewish people had settled in Palestine, the Babylonians from Mesopotamia raided their country and captured Jerusalem. Hundreds of Jews were taken prisoner and transported to Babylon, but they never forgot their God, and longed for the time when they would be set free.

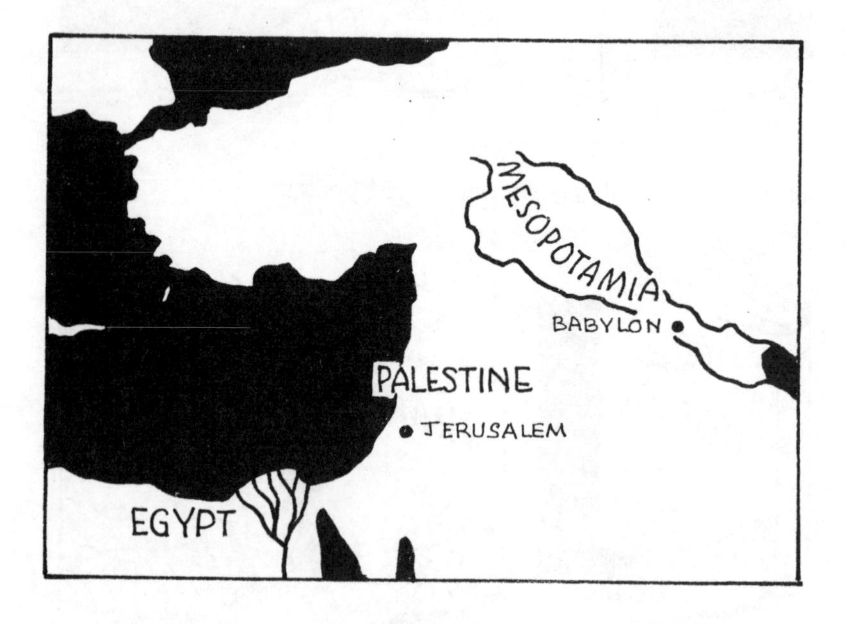


When they did return, they became an even closer community. They were ruled by priests, whose holy building, and the 'centre of government', was the temple in Jerusalem.

When Jesus came, he tried to show the Jewish people a new way of life, where God's kingdom was based on love, and included all people. It was not only for the Jews.

## THE OLD TESTAMENT

When the important stories, laws and history of the Old Testament were at last written down, they were copied again and again over the years. At first they were written on *scrolls*, but from the Second Century AD sheets of parchment were used. Nearly a thousand years after Jesus was born the books were still being copied and written out by hand by *scribes*. As the books were copied, mistakes crept in, so that some of them had altered a great deal from the originals. At last it was decided that one copy, and only one, should be chosen as the 'true writings', and all other copies were destroyed.

In 1947, near the Dead Sea in Israel, some very old scrolls were found. These were some of the old writings that had been hidden, but not actually destroyed, when that decision was made. It was an extremely important discovery, as they were older than any other existing Jewish manuscripts and showed that, in fact, the scribes had done their work well, for the newly-found scrolls did not differ very much from the 'official' books.

Nearly all the Old Testament was written in Hebrew, which the Jewish people spoke before they were carried off to Babylon. When they returned, they began using the Aramaic language, although Hebrew was still taught in the synagogue schools, and spoken in the religious services. Jesus learnt Hebrew as a child although he, too, spoke in the Aramaic language.

Even before Jesus was born, the country of Greece, and its people, began to have a great influence on the Jewish community in Palestine. There was trading and transport and communication between Palestine and Greece, and the Greek language became known and understood. Many Hebrew people began to speak it, and the old writings were translated into Greek for the Jews who spoke Greek. Probably a group of translators met to produce this Greek version, which became known as the *Septuagint*. It was later used by the early Christians.

## THE NEW TESTAMENT

The followers of Jesus, and the very earliest members of the Christian Church, had no idea that their letters and other writings would one day become a collection that we call the New Testament. It was not until nearly 400 years later that the writings were finally put together to form the New Testament as we know it.

By then, the old scrolls on which the letters and books had been written were becoming difficult to store and preserve, and the very first type of book, a *codex*, was produced.

Long before that, the writings had been on papyrus, a crude form of paper made from the papyrus reed, but then vellum, a parchment usually made from calf-skin, was being used.

As Christianity spread, translations from the original Greek manuscripts were made in Latin. Unfortunately, mistakes were made in the translation so, at last, a very learned monk called Jerome was asked by the Pope himself to revise the Latin Testament. This version, still in Latin and completed in 404AD, was called the *Vulgate*.

The Vulgate was used in churches all over Europe for a thousand years. Because it was still in Latin, as most books were in those days, monks were often the only people who could read and understand it. They copied it faithfully, word for word, so that it could be sent to monasteries and churches in all Christian countries.

The ordinary people had to learn the Bible stories from the pictures in their churches, and from their priests. It was not until the 14th Century that the whole Bible was translated into English, and another hundred years before printing was invented. At first, printed Bibles were very expensive, so it was a long time before ordinary people could own Bibles themselves.

# CHURCH MUSIC

Most people feel that they want to worship God not only in words, but in paintings, poetry, drama, dance and music; in fact, in every form of art that we know.

Music has always been associated with worship. Perhaps this is because it can stir up so easily the emotions of the people who perform or listen.

We know that the ancient Egyptians used music for religious purposes. The Israelites, many of whom had lived in Egypt in the early days, made music an important part of their worship, too.

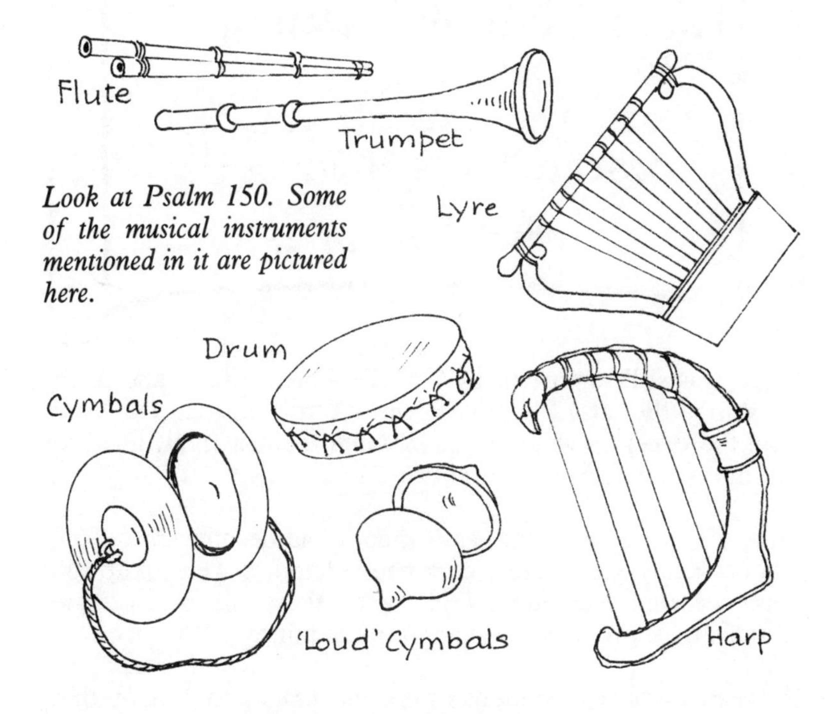


*Look at Psalm 150. Some of the musical instruments mentioned in it are pictured here.*

*You can find out what the harps and lyres were made from by reading 1 Kings 10.12.*

The Jewish people loved processions, and these were accompanied by music and dancing.

O God, your march of triumph
is seen by all,
the procession of God, my king,
into his sanctuary.
The singers are in front, the
musicians are behind,
in between are the girls
beating the tambourines.
'Praise God in the meeting of
his people;
praise the Lord, all you
descendants of Jacob!'

Psalm 68.24-26, GNB

Music was still important in New Testament times, and in the worship of the early Church. The new Christians had also learnt from the Greeks that their music should be just right, in words and mood, for their worship of God.

When Christianity spread, and when it had become an 'official' religion many years later, enormous churches were built, and music became even more important. All special services and festivals were provided with appropriate music.

In the monasteries the monks were encouraged to develop their musical gifts, and much music was composed, particularly to be sung.

The very first organs were used in the churches in Constantinople, which is now Istanbul. In the 8th Century they were introduced into more Westerly churches, but they were so large, and so difficult to play, that they were not often used, and became neglected. Most churches preferred their music to be sung unaccompanied. The singing was often on only one or two notes, and was known as plainsong. (See page 73.)

Until the 16th Century most church music was sung. Harmonising was considered a little unchristian amongst the church leaders; it sounded too much like the music that was performed for people's entertainment.

But at last an Italian composer called Palestrina (1524-1594) was approved of and accepted by the Roman Catholic Church, and he wrote some of the greatest sacred music we know.

There were choirs in most churches, and the *anthem* was developed after the Reformation. The choir sang a special piece, often one of the psalms adapted to new music, and were accompanied by the organ, which had once again become an important part of church music.

Martin Luther was a man who encouraged the people who came to worship in the churches to take an active part in the singing; before this, only the trained choir had been allowed to sing. Luther himself wrote hymns and music for them.

By the 17th Century the Protestant churches had choirs which were often accompanied by instruments other than the organ. A great German composer, Johann Sebastian Bach, wrote music not only for the usual church services but also long, impressive pieces for the organ and for other instruments. These were performed to the glory of God in many of Europe's finest cathedrals.

*Try to find out the names of some of these pieces. Borrow a cassette tape or a record so that you can hear for yourself some of Bach's great music.*

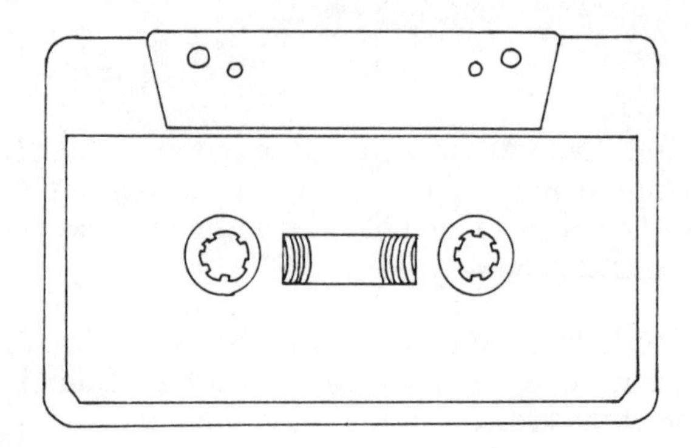

After Bach, composers such as Haydn, Mozart and Beethoven also wrote sacred music, but these were more for church 'concerts', although they all had religious themes.

*Oratorios*, which were dramatic musicals of biblical passages or stories, were first written in Italy in the 17th Century. They were performed in churches, often with scenery and costumes. Later, they were written for, and performed in, concert halls. Large choirs took part, and were accompanied by famous orchestras. George Frederick Handel wrote his great oratorio *The Messiah* about this time, and King George I attended a performance of it in London.

In the 18th Century a great number of hymns were written, and many of them are still sung today. Some, however, now seem very 'dated' and sentimental, and are being left out of many new and revised hymnbooks.

At the beginning of the 20th Century people again began to write special music for part of a church service. Ralph Vaughan Williams and Benjamin Britten are among the best-known composers of these works.

Since then, there have been some 'pop' musicals on religious themes written and performed on stage and for films including *Godspell*, *Jesus Christ Superstar*, and *Joseph and the Amazing Technicolour Dreamcoat*.

Nowadays, music still plays an important part in our church services, and there are new musicals being written every year. Roger Jones, a modern composer, has written several, including *From Pharaoh to Freedom*, which tells the story of the Jewish Passover, and *Saints Alive!*, the story of Pentecost. There are many others, too, and new, exciting carols and hymns, for voices, guitars and recorders.

# THE HYMNS WE SING

People have always shown their joy in singing and in music. It is a natural way of praising God.

In Old Testament times the Hebrews praised God by singing psalms in the synagogues and in the temple.

Here is a psalm of joy and praising:

Sing to the Lord, all the world!
Worship the Lord with joy;
come before him with happy songs!

Acknowledge that the Lord is God.
He made us, and we belong to him;
we are his people, we are his flock.

Enter the temple gates with
thanksgiving,
go into its courts with praise.
Give thanks to him and
praise him.

The Lord is good;
his love is eternal
and his faithfulness lasts
for ever.

Psalm 100 (GNB)

Jesus and his disciples learnt the psalms when they were very young, and loved to sing them. In Matthew 26.30 it is recorded that, after the last supper, they all sang a hymn, which was probably a psalm, before going out to the Mount of Olives.

After Jesus died and rose again, the first Christians still worshipped in the synagogues, so it is not surprising that they went on singing the old psalms.

Paul and Silas, who took the Good News of Jesus to people far away, were often in trouble for what they were doing.

We are told that they sang hymns of joy even when they were in prison (Acts 16.25).

We are not told whether these hymns were versions of the psalms, but later Paul wrote:

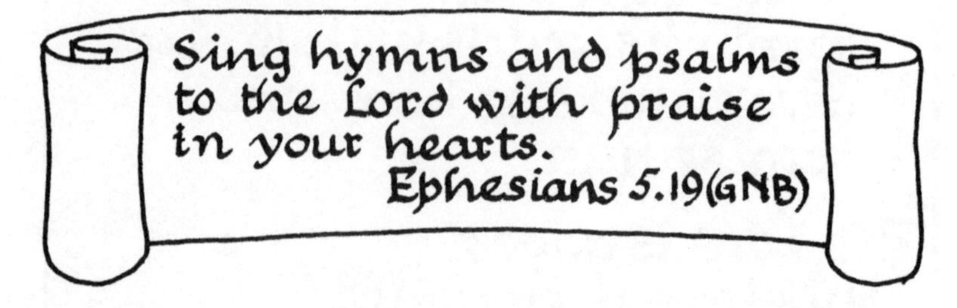


So it seems that, by that time, a hymn and a psalm were two different things. The words quoted by Paul in Ephesians 5.14 may also have been the words from one of the very first Christian hymns.

There are no records of any hymns which had definite rhythm or poetry, like the ones we know, for another 300 years.

One of the earliest hymns we know of is still sung in churches today. You may be able to find it in your church hymnbook:

'Hail, gladdening Light'
or
'O gladsome Light'.

This was probably written about 300AD, but it may have been even earlier. Many years later it was translated from Greek into English. One translator was John Keble, another John Mason Neale.

In medieval times, many of the monks in France had once been *troubadours*, men who entertained by singing and reciting poetry at the French Court.

When they entered the monasteries, to give their lives to God, they began to write poetry that could be set to music and sung in the abbeys. They wrote in Latin, but John Mason Neale translated some of the oldest poems into English.

You must know this one →

All glory,
laud, and
honour
to thee,
Redeemer,
King!
to whom the lips
of children made
sweet hosannas
ring.

At about the time when the monks were singing the first hymns, Pope Gregory I introduced what we call *plainsong* into the churches and monasteries.

Plainsong consisted of Latin words set to a 'plain' kind of music. They did not rhyme and had no metre. Many monasteries and convents and some churches still sing plainsong chants today.

*See if you can find a record or cassette of some plainsong, and listen to its sounds.*

In Great Britain there were very few hymns sung before the 17th Century. Poets wrote sacred poems, but they were not often set to music, and were published in papers and books to be read privately.

Some of these have now been set to music, and we sing them today. One of them is 'Teach me, my God and King', written by the poet George Herbert. 'Let us with a gladsome mind' is another, written by John Milton and based on Psalm 136.

All this time people still sang psalms in the churches, but hymns were rarely sung until late in the 17th Century, when they began to be written specially to be sung by the congregation.

Christmas and Easter carols, however, had been sung for hundreds of years. They had been one way in which the ordinary people could express their praise, in their own language, at the great festival times of the Church.

Before hymns were sung in churches the services were often long and boring, so people welcomed the chance to sing. Many hymns told Bible stories, and many gave teaching about living in God's way.

Here are two of the earliest hymn writers, with examples of the hymns they gave the people:

And this is how just one hymn came to be written.

Henry Lyte had written the hymn-'Abide with me...' in one evening. Today it is a favourite with many people. The music he wrote has been lost, but the words are known all over the world.

Women also began to write hymns, many of which you probably know and sing today.

*Look through hymnbooks and make a list of your favourite hymns.*

New hymns are still being written, in the kind of speech we use every day. Nowadays we do not often use the words 'thee' and 'thou' when singing. What do we use instead?

Many of the old tunes, too, have been replaced by good modern ones. Do you know the 'new' tunes for the hymns:
'O Jesus, I have promised'
'Holy, holy, holy'?

Hymns are not out of date; they are not all ancient. There must be modern expressions of praise and prayer suitable for the modern age.

Whatever we sing in church or chapel, or at any place where Christians meet together, it must be the best that all of us — writers, musicians and singers — can offer to God.

It was hot and sticky in the prison cell, and the walls were running with moisture. Dr Kao tried to sleep, but the night was filled with the noises of insects flying free outside. It was a long time since he had walked free in the night air. Dr Kao was no criminal; all he had done was to help an innocent fugitive find a place to hide in Taipei, and for this the authorities had sentenced him to seven years' imprisonment.

As Dr Kao lay there he thought of hymns he knew. Sometimes new words and music came into his mind, and he later told how one of these hymns came to be written:

'On the night of July 31st, 1983 I was asleep and had a dream. I saw many people who were singing. As they sang they became more and more joyous. It seemed that life was overflowing from within them. Suddenly I awoke and pondered the dream. I got up from my pallet and began to write. After words came to me I felt God giving me a melody, which I recorded on paper. The hymn with — words and melody — were completed that evening and given to my wife Ruth during her next visit to the prison.

The hymn was entitled "O Lord, You are the Life of the World".'

At last Dr Kao was released. He had suffered a great deal, but was able to say that Christ, the 'Life of the World', had given him strength to face everything with courage and cheerfulness.

# O LORD, YOU ARE THE LIFE OF THE WORLD

O Lord, you are the life of the world.
O Lord, you are the life of the world.
Live within me and enrich me
until I live like you.

O Lord, make me a lamp of new life.
O Lord, make me a lamp of new life
in the darkest suffering places;
make me shine always.

O Lord, make me a spring of new life.
O Lord, make me a spring of new life
for the thirsty crying people;
keep me flowing ever.

SCRIPT OF MARK 3.35, IN TAIWAN

# CHURCH DRAMA

From very early times the Greeks and Romans performed plays in front of audiences, and in the time of Jesus there were many grand amphitheatres in Palestine. Plays were staged there for the annual festivals of the Roman gods. When the Roman Empire collapsed, theatres, and the writing of plays, declined.

We next read of plays being performed in the ninth century, but it was not until the Middle Ages that the Church took the lead in drama, finding that acting was a very good way to teach people Bible stories. Church services were said in Latin by the priests, but the teaching plays were performed by ordinary people speaking their own language.

Soon, there were so many 'spectators' that the plays became mobile. The *Mystery Plays* were mounted on Pageant Wagons which went through the towns, stopping at various vantage points. The stories the actors told, of Noah, Abraham and Isaac, the birth of Jesus, and his resurrection, were all spoken in the easily understood 'chatter' of working men and women.

Gradually the craft guilds in the towns took over the responsibility, and the honour, of producing a play at Festival times. York, Coventry and Chester were all well known for their Mystery Plays, and people from the surrounding towns and villages flocked into the cities to see them. Even visiting royalty and the local noblemen watched the plays from windows in the wealthy houses.

The actors had to be very dramatic and colourful to gain the attention of the noisy crowds, especially as the plays were very long. One performed in York in 1415 began at 4 o'clock in the morning and went on until 9 o'clock at night! Today a Mystery Play is still performed each year in York, based on the medieval cycle of plays, but now lasting only three hours.

Trace and colour this picture

By the end of the 16th century, Mystery Plays, others called Miracle Plays (mostly about saints), and Morality Plays, were no longer performed. But they had made the way ready for everyone to enjoy other forms of theatrical drama.

In Bavaria a spectacular biblical drama is performed every ten years by the villagers of Oberammergau. It began in 1634. The previous year the villagers had been spared from a plague. As thanks to God, they decided to act out the suffering of Jesus in a play. Everyone in the village was involved — as they still are today. People now travel from all over the world to see the play.

Much later, the Bible was used in the making of films — there were so many good and dramatic happenings recorded in it that could be used to draw big audiences. One of the first to be filmed was *Samson and Delilah*, made before sound came to the cinema.

Huge crowds were paid to act, and enormous sets were built for the biblical epics which followed, such as *The Greatest Story Ever Told* and *King of Kings*.

We have had stage plays too, like *Godspell* and *Jesus Christ Superstar*, both musicals with modern music which were later made into films.

Churches have had many performances of biblical plays, with ordinary members of the congregation taking part. Often the only scenery has been the setting of the church itself. In some churches dance, as a form of religious drama, is regularly performed, and hymns and songs are brought up to date with the accompaniment of modern band groups and orchestras.

On page 70 you can read of three new musicals specially written to be performed by Christian groups.

Many churches have their own drama groups which perform all types of plays and musicals, both in their churches and in halls in their communities. In a South London Borough all the churches in the neighbourhood, of every denomination, take part in a drama competition every year.

And at Christmas the nativity story is dramatised in hundreds of churches by children and adults; the story of Christmas is told again and again to the ordinary people to remind them what Christmas really means.

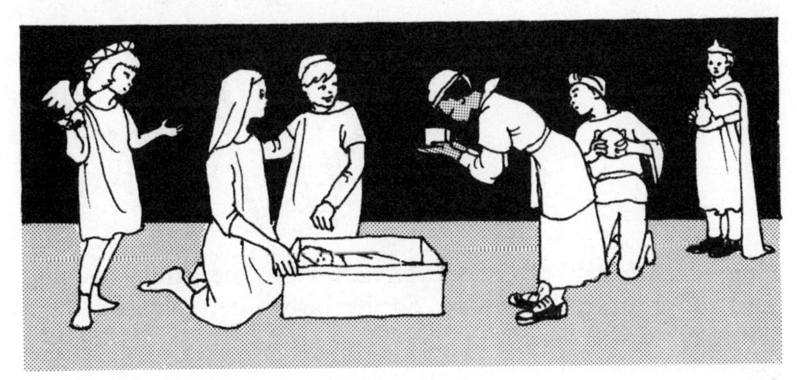

# TO CHURCH ON SUNDAY

To the Jews, the Sabbath was a very special day. It was the 'seventh day' which they believed God had set aside for rest and worship.

In the old story of creation we read:

> He (God) blessed the seventh day and set it apart as a special day, because by that day he had completed his creation and stopped working.
>
> (Genesis 2.3, GNB)

When the Jewish laws were drawn up, one of them stated:

> You have six days in which to do your work, but remember that the seventh day, the Sabbath, is a day of rest. On that day do not work, but gather for worship. The Sabbath belongs to the Lord, no matter where you live.
>
> (Leviticus 23.3, GNB)

This 'seventh day' extended from sunset on the Friday evening until sunset on the Saturday. So the Jewish holy day became a Saturday.

To foreigners, like the Romans who occupied Palestine at the time of Jesus, it seemed that the Jews, by keeping the Sabbath as a rest day, were lazy, and wasteful with their time.

One Roman, called Seneca, who lived at the same time as Jesus, wrote of the Jews:

But it was only *one* day. Today most people, in the Western world at least, take two whole days off each week — Saturday and Sunday. Many of them do not realise that the week-end was established in the beginning for religious reasons, those of the Jews and the Christians.

The first Christians were also Jews, so they naturally went along to their synagogues on the Sabbath day. But they also remembered the words that Jesus had spoken:

The first Jewish Christians did not observe all the very strict Jewish rules about work and fasting on the Sabbath day, and gradually they began to think it would be better if they had their own holy day, one that would be special to the Christians alone.

They chose Sunday, the first day of the week. It was the day when Jesus had risen from the dead. At first it was known as *The Lord's Day* and was a day of rejoicing, when a meal was shared by the whole Christian community in a town. This meal usually ended with sharing round bread and wine, in memory of the Last Supper. It was also a day when new Christians came to be baptised.

However, it was not until the Roman Emperor Constantine became a Christian that Sunday *laws* were brought in, and Christians were actually forbidden to work on a Sunday.

Over the years the Church rules for what could or could not be done on a Sunday became almost as restricting as the old Jewish Sabbath laws had been. By the time of the Puritans, Sunday had become a day when nothing could be done that was not religious in some way. Everybody *had* to go to church, and all work, games and unnecessary travelling had to stop.

In 1677 a law was passed by Parliament, called the *Act of Sunday Observance*, which set down exactly what was allowed and what was not allowed on the 'day of rest'. Sunday laws, often disputed, still exist.

Most Christians try to attend a church service on a Sunday. They still feel that it is a day of rest, which should in some way be different from the rest of the week. By going to church they set aside time to worship in the company of other Christians, and this has become, for them, a time of refreshment and rejoicing, just as it was in the days of the early Church.

*Look at church notice-boards and magazines. What times are the most popular for holding Sunday services? Are there any churches that hold weekday services as well? And what meetings are there during the week for the different age groups of people who go to the church?*

# SAINTS AND SAINTS' DAYS

## Who are the Saints?

People who have led exceptionally holy lives have sometimes been officially recognised by the Church as saints — not during their lifetime, but often many, many years afterwards. Some of them were martyrs, put to death for the sake of the Gospel. Others performed heroic or famous deeds, had visions, or did miraculous things. Some were ordinary people, living in quiet towns or villages, some were kings or queens, but all of them lived such good lives that they were remembered and revered.

In St Paul's day all those who believed in Christ and followed him were called 'Saints'. *Read Romans 1.7 in the Authorised Version or Revised Standard Version of the Bible. Then read the same verse in the Good News Bible to see how the word 'Saints' has been changed.*

## The first Saints

The first people to be 'made' saints were early Christian martyrs. The first person we hear of in the Bible who died because he was a follower of Christ is Stephen — *St Stephen*. He was murdered by his fellow-Jews for daring to stand up and point out how wrong they had been for years.

The Romans also persecuted the early Christians: these first members of the early Church would not keep quiet, they would not even stay in one place. Perhaps if Christ's friends and followers had 'sensibly' and quietly kept their faith to themselves, they might have been safer.

But they would also be completely unknown in the world today. Christianity would simply not exist!

The Romans were constantly tracking down these Christians and taking them prisoners in far-off places of the Roman Empire, as well as persecuting them in the towns of Palestine. The Christians were like water from a river that had overflowed its banks, getting into every nook and cranny of the Empire. This made the Empire, and the Emperor himself, feel uneasy and threatened.

So, after Stephen, many Christians were put to death, often after the most dreadful tortures imaginable. Saints, men and women, were in the making, as Christian after Christian was murdered.

Many years afterwards, when the Church was established and official, people remembered these early martyrs, and *canonised* those who could be named: that is, they were officially made *saints*. A few of these early saints, killed by the Romans, were St Apolline (see page 90), St Martina, St Cletus, and St Alphius.

The Church also venerated those who had worked with Jesus, like St Peter, St Andrew, St James and St John, and those who had had contact with him, like St Mary of Magdala, St Simon of Cyrene (who helped to carry Jesus' cross), and Longinus (the Roman soldier who was at the foot of the cross when Jesus died).

St Peter, by Mantegna

## BECOMING A SAINT

Some parts of the Church continue to make holy people 'saints'. Other Christians say that *all* faithful believers are saints and that the Church cannot judge between them.

Every country has its own saints. One British saint was *Ninian*, who went to Rome to study and become a bishop. He then returned to Scotland and preached Christianity to the Picts. He founded an important monastery from where he did his missionary work. He died about the year 432AD.

## RECOGNISING THE SAINTS

Pictures, statues, and symbols help people to remember the various saints; many wall paintings (murals) and early oil paintings tell the stories of their lives. Many of the paintings and statues are not labelled or named, but objects reminding us of a particular person help to identify him or her.

St Apolline, who was martyred by the Romans in about 249AD, is always recognised by the very large pincers she holds in which can be seen a tooth. It was said that Apolline had been tortured by having all her teeth pulled out! She is now called the patron saint of dentists! There is a tiny 14th Century chapel in Guernsey dedicated to her.

Similarly, St Patrick is easily recognised by the shamrock he holds; St Francis of Assisi is always surrounded by birds and animals; and St Catherine of Alexandria by a wheel, which shows the way she was tortured before her death.

We are still reminded of St Catherine every year on Bonfire Night; can you say how?

## SAINTS' DAYS

It became the custom over the years to remember and honour these holy people on certain days of the year, usually on the day of their death.

In the early days, every Saint's Day became a festival, a day's holiday, until by the Middle Ages there were so many Feast Days that work of all kinds was being seriously neglected and interrupted. So the Pope decided that the number of Saints' Days must be reduced. Many more days have since been officially done away with, and as recently as 1969 the Pope again reduced them, and selected only a few that must be celebrated by the Roman Catholic Church.

Some feast days are still public holidays. In Ireland, for instance, St Patrick's Day is a holiday — 17th March.

St George's Day, St Andrew's Day, and St David's Day are still remembered in Britain.

*Find out the dates of these special days.*

The Union Jack

Which saints should we think of when we see this flag?

Today there are many people who work for Christ, all over the world, serving him among the poor, the starving, and the homeless. They are not perfect people, but they live their lives reflecting Christ on earth, doing their best to carry his message of love and compassion to all people.

Hundreds of them are unknown, and will never be named, or celebrated, but they are today's true saints of God.

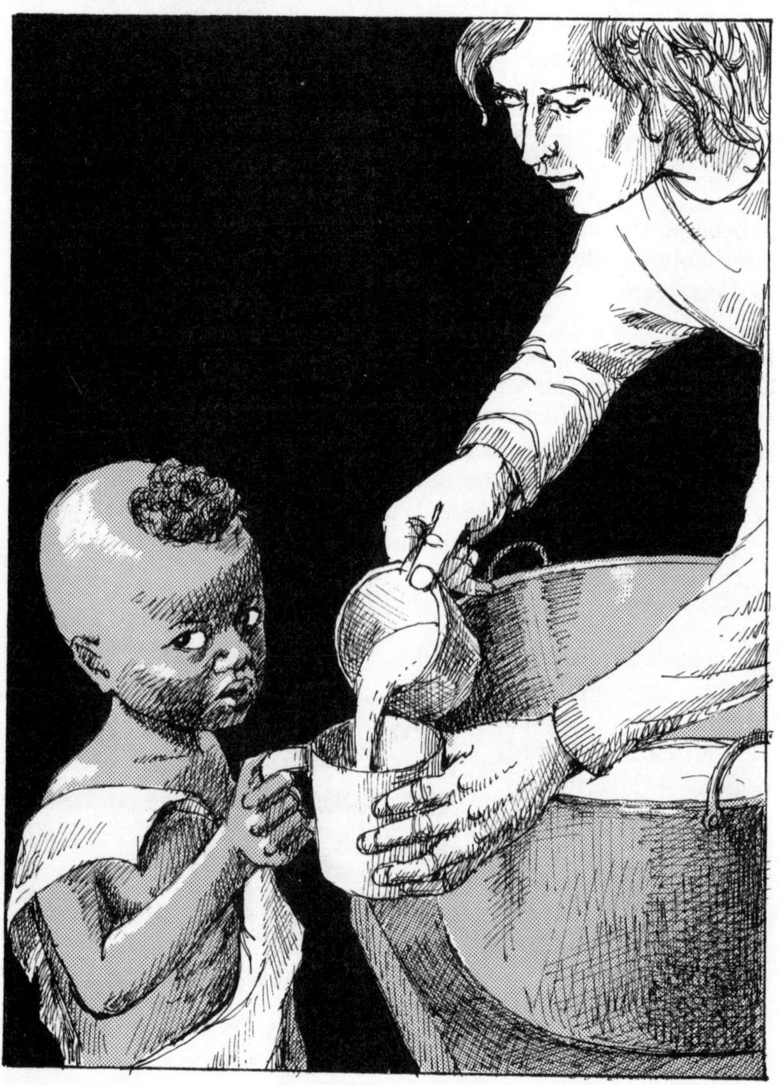

# THE STORY OF ST STEPHEN

(The full story of Stephen can be found in Acts 6 and 7.)

Boxing Day, 26th December, is also the Feast Day of St Stephen. He was the man we think of as the first Christian martyr.

Stephen was a man who was strong in the faith, who firmly believed that the Holy Spirit gave Christ's followers great courage and power, and who was a leader in the early Church. He was one of seven men elected to be in charge of the distribution of money, a kind of treasurer.

Stephen was a learned man, so he also took an active part in representing the other Christians, and speaking up for them. Because of this, he got into an argument with some Jews who attended a synagogue in the city of Jerusalem. Once he started speaking to them, they found they could not get the better of him. Their only chance of 'winning' the argument was to convince the synagogue elders and teachers that he was spreading malicious rumours about the Jews' holy temple.

They bribed unscrupulous men to go to the elders saying that they had heard Stephen say that Jesus would destroy the temple and change all the ancient laws of Moses. Stephen was taken to court. He was asked if the charge against him was true and, for his reply, he gave a speech which is recorded in Acts 7.2-53.

Herod's Temple

*Read parts of it.*

Stephen was obviously a well-educated man who knew his Jewish history and scriptures well. He argued that there was no building, whether it was the temple, a synagogue or a church, that could actually be called the residence of God. Stephen was forceful; he was outspoken and brave.

'How stubborn you are!' he cried in court to the Jewish elders and priests. 'How deaf you are to God's message! All through history you have killed anyone who tried to bring you God's word. You didn't listen when they said that God would send a Messiah to show people the right and good way to live. And now you have murdered the Messiah who came! He was here with you — God's messenger himself — and you executed him!'

Stephen hardly noticed the anger on the council members' faces, or heard the muttering in court.

The Christian witnesses saw it and heard it, though, and were fearful for Stephen's safety. There he was, looking up as if the power to speak this way, the power of the Holy Spirit, was coming directly from God. It was as if he could see Jesus himself!

The Council had had enough. No one wanted to hear any more. There was no waiting for a verdict, no judgement, no sentencing.

Stephen was mobbed in court, and hustled out by the seething council members. He was dragged through the city streets, out through the city gates, and hurled to the ground.
People were already lobbing stones at him, and violence broke out. Men stripped off their coats and cloaks and left them in charge of a young man, Saul, before rushing to join in stoning the man who had dared to stand up to them in court.

There was no hope that Stephen would survive; everyone was in a frenzy of hate, and wanted his death.

'Lord Jesus,' Stephen called, 'receive my spirit!' Then, on his knees, he still had the strength to shout, 'Lord! Do not remember this sin against them!' He was asking God to forgive the very people who were killing him.

Very soon it was all over. The mob went off, leaving Stephen on the ground, stoned to death.

Trace and colour this picture of Stephen's death.

# THE TRINITY

'The grace of our Lord Jesus Christ, the love of God, and the fellowship of the Holy Spirit, be with us all, evermore.'

Do you ever say these words in church, or at school, or perhaps at your youth club or organisation? The prayer is usually called *The Grace*, and most Christian people, from whatever church they come, know the words by heart.

The prayer was first written by St Paul, at the end of his second letter to the church in Corinth (2 Corinthians 13.13).

The prayer speaks of three things:
the grace of Jesus Christ,
the love of God,
and the fellowship of the Holy Spirit.

The words are almost a formula; they express what Christians believe in, and their understanding of God: God the Father, Christ the Saviour, and the Holy Spirit — God in three persons. This is called the *Trinity*, or 'three in one'.

In the very early days the Christian Church needed to explain to outsiders what the Church was and what it believed in. It is not always easy to put such things into words; people were confused, and this led to much discussion and argument.

It took 400 years for exact words of belief to be decided upon, but at last a *creed* was formed, called the *Nicene Creed*.

Today, the Nicene Creed is said in many churches all over the world at Communion Services. It is a simple statement of Christian belief, and it includes these words:

We believe in one God,
the Father, the almighty . . .
We believe in one Lord, Jesus Christ,
the only Son of God . . .
We believe in the Holy Spirit,
the Lord, the giver of life . . .

Pictures have always been helpful in explaining things, and the Trinity is sometimes pictured like this:

You may know and sing the hymn:

'Holy, holy, holy, Lord God almighty'.

Look again at the first and last verses. The hymn is all about the Trinity.

St Patrick once needed to explain the Trinity to some fierce chieftains. He found that they could not understand the words he was saying, and he had nothing to draw a picture on. So he bent down and picked a shamrock leaf, which is very much like a clover leaf.

Shamrocks grow in Ireland; it would be difficult to find one growing wild in England, Wales or Scotland. *If you had to explain the Trinity to someone, and had no shamrock or clover leaves around, can you think of any other 'three part' things that you could use to illustrate this?*

# CHURCH VESTMENTS

A *vestment* is an official dress or robe. Sometimes the Queen wears vestments; so does a duke, or an earl, or a Lord Mayor. Vestments are not ordinary, everyday clothes, but those worn when people are 'on duty' at official functions. They are the clothes by which we can recognise their position.

Most clergy wear special clothes when they are 'on duty'. Many of the robes worn by Roman Catholic and Anglican priests are similar to those worn by bishops and priests when the Christian Church was first officially recognised, in the 4th Century.

At first the priests wore robes that were the same as those worn by wealthy Romans. But fashion in dress does not last very long, and the Romans changed their styles. The Church officials, however, did not change the style of what they wore, and kept to the early Roman costume right up to the time of the Reformation.

When people broke away from the Roman Catholic Church, and formed the Protestant Church, they thought that the dress of the clergy should be simpler. Much of the richness in dress has now returned, especially in the Anglican Church.

People in Roman times wore a long white tunic for everyday wear. This was called a *linea*. Because it was always white, we now call the linea worn by clergy the *alb*, which means white. (Think of *albumen*, the white of an egg, or *albino*, an all-white animal or person, or an *albatross*, a white bird.) Priests still wear a long white tunic, called the alb, under a *chasuble* at Communion services.

Over the alb priests wore a *stole*, a long scarf of rich silk, hanging down at the front. Different coloured stoles are worn according to the Church seasons:

purple for Advent and Lent, white and gold for Christmas and Easter, green for Epiphany and the Sundays after Pentecost, and red for Pentecost and Saints' Days. (The cloths hanging from the pulpit and lectern, and often the altar cloth, are also changed to match the Church seasons.) The stole may be tied at the waist by a girdle.

The Romans covered their long white linea tunics with a large loose cloak called a *casula* when they went out, or for very special occasions indoors. This has become the *chasuble* which covers the priest's alb today. It is often richly decorated with embroidery.

A bishop wears a special 'hat' called a *mitre*. It is thought that the first Christian bishops copied the shape of the Old Testament High Priest's headwear, which was tall and made of white linen. Over the years this has developed into the present shape. Celtic bishops used to wear a golden crown instead of a mitre.

After the Reformation, a much simpler dress was approved of by the Church of England. This is still worn by vicars and priests as an alternative for the normal Sunday services, although the chasuble is used for Communion services, and by bishops at their services. The alb was replaced by a shorter white gown, a *surplice* with wide sleeves.

A *cassock* is also an alternative form of dress, worn every day by some priests and nonconformist ministers. It is a long — usually black — gown. The clergy in hot countries usually wear an alb, and this white gown is becoming popular all over the world.

Cassocks are also worn in many churches and cathedrals by members of the choir. The cassocks are often rich in colour and are sometimes covered by a very short surplice called a *cotta*.

Many clergymen wear *dog-collars*, a white back-to-front collar over a shirt-front usually coloured black, grey or blue. These have been worn since the 19th Century when they replaced the neck-cloth worn by gentlemen.

For many years women had to be content with serving the Church and its people in very humble ways, leaving the leading and preaching to men. But nowadays there are women ministers in many Nonconformist churches, and Anglicans allow women to take a greater part in ministry than before. Ordained women have similar vestments to the men, although some prefer to wear simple, ordinary dress.

Many church people now question whether it is necessary for the clergy to wear 'special' clothes at all. To some, such vestments seem out of place and ornate in the modern world.

There are churchgoers, however, who find them useful to the atmosphere of worship, and would not like any change. A dog-collar also helps a clergyman to be recognised in the community. But some ministers find it more helpful to people if they are not dressed in 'official' clothes.

*Ask people who go to church what they think: do they like to see their priests and ministers in special clothing?*

# CHRISTIAN SIGNS AND SYMBOLS

When you see a *cross*, it reminds you of Christianity, for Jesus died on a cross. This is the best-known symbol of the Church.

An empty cross makes people think of the risen Christ.

A *crucifix* is a cross which has a figure of Jesus on it. This reminds people of his great love in dying for them.

There are many other crosses which have connections with the Christian faith, but the best known is the simplest, like the one above.

Some churches are built in the shape of a cross, with the window above the altar pointing to the east, towards Israel, the place where Jesus was born.

Very old Norman churches often used a cross like this one which we now call a *Maltese Cross*. Sometimes it was enclosed in a circle.

A cross like this was also used by the Christian Knights in the days of the Crusades. It can still be seen as part of the St John Ambulance Brigade's badge.

The *Celtic Cross* is a cross with a circle added to it. It was often mounted on a stone pillar. Ones that are still seen today are often rubbed almost smooth by the weather, but when they were first erected their beautiful and complicated carving could be clearly seen.

*Trace and colour this celtic pattern, which is like one used for the very centre of an old cross in Scotland.*

Stone crosses were often placed outside churches or in churchyards, or on the village green, and were used to mark places where monks and priests gathered the people together to hear Bible stories.

There is a very old stone cross in the churchyard in Whalley in Lancashire. It indicates that there was a Christian church on the site long before the present church was built.

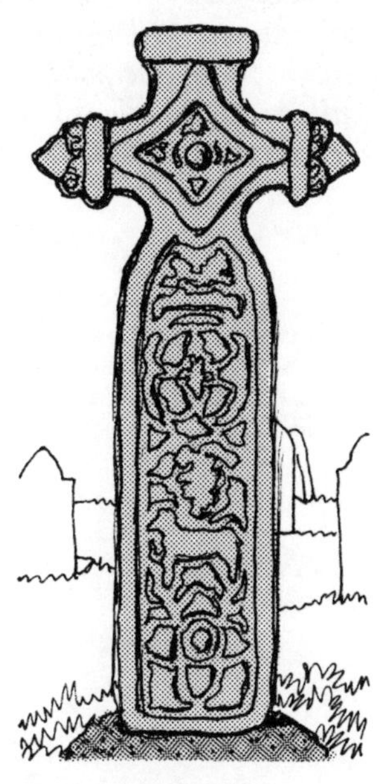

Some of these stone crosses had large crucifixes fixed to them originally, but nearly all these crucifixes were destroyed at the time of the Reformation. Some of them were replaced by sundials, including those which can be seen at Checkley in Staffordshire, Eyam in Derbyshire, and Laleston in Glamorgan.

A cross mounted on three stone steps is called a *Calvary Cross*. The three steps symbolise faith, hope and love. *Have you seen quite modern crosses, often used as war memorials, mounted in this way?*

Inside churches are many more symbolic crosses, signs of Christ.

*See how many you can find in your own church, perhaps on a Bible or hymnbook, on the pulpit, hung on a wall or in an alcove. There may even be one on the notice-board.*

Beautiful gold crosses, carried high on long poles, are taken into some churches when the priest enters. These are called *Processional Crosses*, and are a symbol of the way Christ leads his people.

Some crosses are very simple indeed. They may be made of wooden poles or planks. Some like this are used to lead modern processions round a town or village, and are followed by Christians from many different churches in the neighbourhood.

One simple cross stands in Coventry Cathedral. It is a replica of three large nails found in the ruins of the bombed cathedral after a night air raid in the Second World War. The nails were bound together to make a cross.

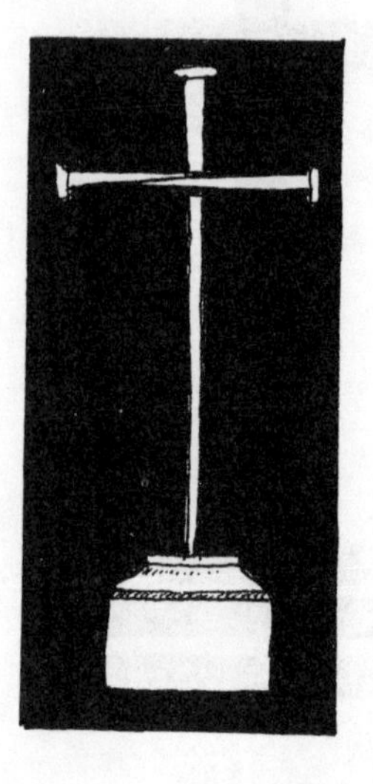

Many churches have cloth (called a *fall*) hanging from the pulpit or lectern (reading desk). Sometimes these are embroidered with a cross, but often have the letters IHS on them. These are the first three letters of the Latin form of the word *Jesus*.

In the Greek language, the first two letters of the word *Christ* are X and P. They are put together as a monogram, and are known as *Chi-rho*. Monograms like this were carved on the catacomb walls by the very early Christians, and the sign also became known as the Emperor Constantine's 'victory sign' at the time when he became a Christian.

Nowadays some people wear Chi-rho badges as a symbol that they follow Christ.

The fish was another very early sign by which Christians knew each other, and which is still used today. It came from the first letters, in Greek, of the words 'Jesus Christ, Son of God, Saviour', which spelt *Ichthus*, a fish.

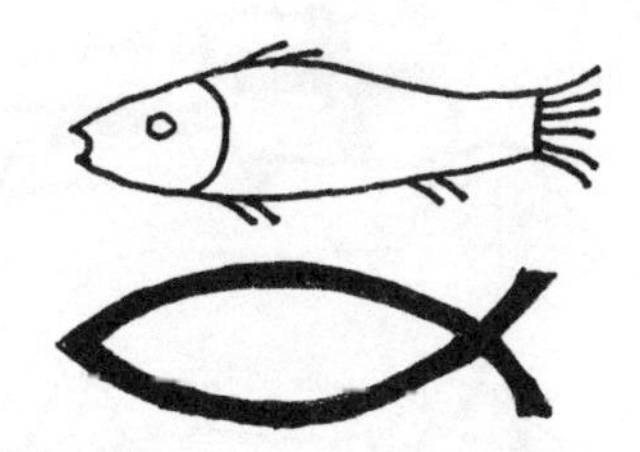

*Look for people wearing fish badges; they will be Christians.*

There are many other Christian symbols, which can be seen in churches and cathedrals all over the country. They are used in stained glass windows, in carvings, or in pictures.

*Here are some symbols. Look up the reference in your Bible to find out how they became Christian symbols, and what they stand for. A church where you may see each of them is also given, but there are many more in other churches. Keep looking for them.*

**The dove**
Reference: Mark 1.10-11.
You can see a dove on the font in a church in Kirkburn, Yorkshire.

A dove is also used as the symbol of

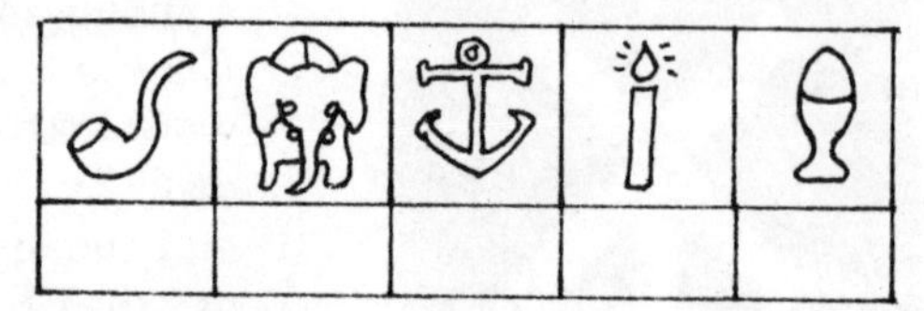

**Keys**
These are the symbol of one of Jesus' disciples.
Reference: Matthew 16.18-19.
The keys represent

St . . . . .

There is a shield with this saint's keys in York Minster.

**A lamb**
Reference: John 1.29.
Remind yourself, as well, of the story of the good shepherd, in Luke 15.4-7.
There is a carved lamb on the end of one of the benches, or pews, in the Parish Church in South Brent, Devonshire.
When the lamb is carrying a *vexillum*, or banner, this reminds us of Christ's triumph over death.

**A crown of thorns**
Reference: John 19.1-3.
There is a very striking crown of thorns used like a screen in the modern Coventry Cathedral.

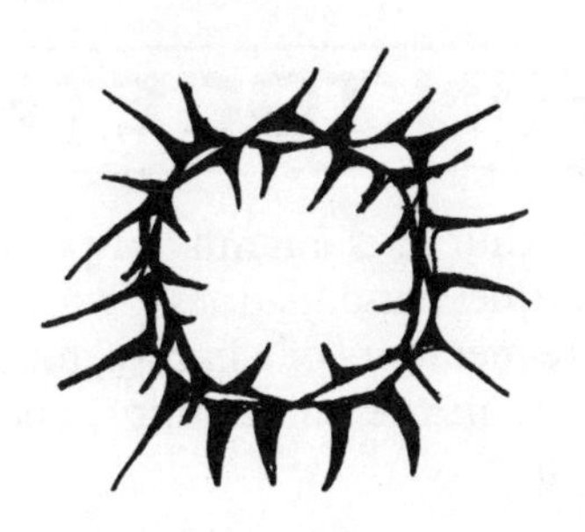

**Interlaced triangles or circles**
Reference: Matthew 28.19.
Have you heard the expression 'God, the three in one'? This is also known as the *Trinity*. (See page 96.)
Look for something like this in stained glass in Cirencester Church.

**A cock**
Reference: John 18.25-27.
A cock can also signify watchfulness, keeping alert for Christ.
Many churches have cocks on weather vanes. Look for them. There is one at Narborough near Leicester.

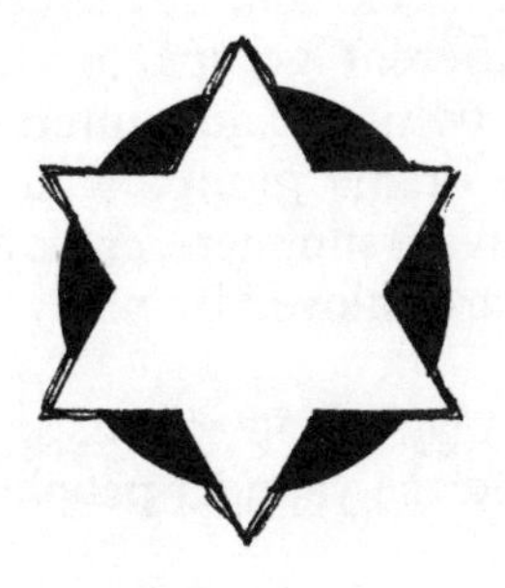

**A star**
Reference: Matthew 2.1-2.
There is a single star on a *boss* (a carving in wood where sections of the ceiling meet) at Tewkesbury Abbey.

# FUN TOGETHER

The church is a family of people and, like all families, has times of sadness and gladness, work and play, solemnity and laughter. Like members of a family, too, the people of the church mix with others in the community, and are glad to share their fun with them.

Let's look at how one church does this, then you can discover when, and how, *your* church members meet together, and share in the fun of the community.

This church — we'll call it the Markham Road United Reformed Church — has fun. After the Sunday morning service, everyone is invited to have coffee and a chat together in one of the church halls.

The coffee is prepared and served by a different group of people each week. Young and old gather to get to know each other better, and to welcome visitors.

During the week church members meet in different groups to share various activities and interests. There is a drama group, a music club, and, in the summer, tennis and swimming are enjoyed by many.

Sometimes the drama group puts on a play for all to see, and a recently formed rock band has interested the younger people.

Occasionally, on fine Sunday afternoons, a church walk-and-picnic is arranged so that members can get to know each other better in a very informal way.

Sometimes the local churches join in with the activities of Markham Road URC. The women from the Baptist Church are invited to the women's Handwork Club lunch, and Markham Road ladies visit the Baptist Church for tea parties and special festivities.

Christians should always be friendly people, and this will show in the way they talk to, and join in the fun of, people they meet at school and work, or in organisations such as the local St John Ambulance Brigade and Old People's clubs. Through the friendship, kindness and caring of Christians, other people may wonder what makes church-goers so happy, and come along to find out.

Markham Road URC has many, many more social activities . . . *Now begin to make a list of all those that go on within your own church.*

# HOW TO MAKE A POSTER FOR A CHURCH EVENT

Your church or youth group may be going to hold a special event, and this needs to be advertised. Sometimes it needs more than a small typed notice on a board or in the magazine, so why not offer to make a poster that would be large enough to be seen by more people?

**You will need:**
Rough paper, two pencils, an elastic band, bold coloured felt-tip pens or poster paint, and a piece of paper (white or coloured) for the finished poster.

## Follow this plan for making your poster:

**1** On the rough paper, write down all the details of the event.

**2** Now decide which is the most important item on that list, because this will need to be the largest and most attractive.

**3** Put the other items in order of importance and cross out unnecessary information.

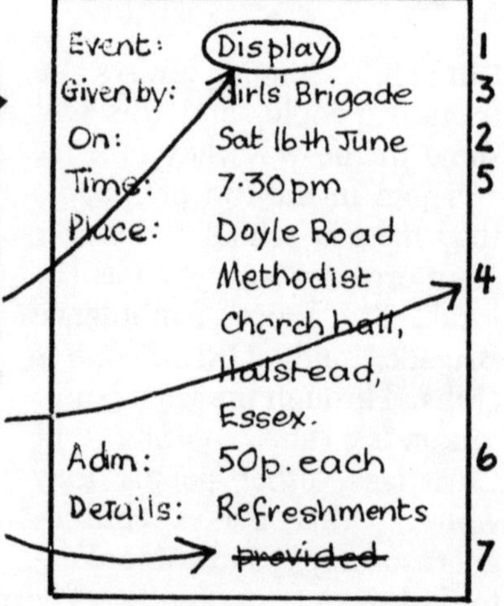


On the rough here, we could cross out the word *Essex*; people likely to come to the Display will know that Halstead is in Essex — they live there! You do not even need words like *on* and *by*, so leave them out, too.

**4** Now, still using rough paper, plan what you expect the finished poster to look like. Remember, a poster always needs to look *balanced*. It need not be completely symmetrical, but a piece of information on the left, for instance, needs to be balanced by something else on the right.

**5** You should now transfer your rough plan onto the larger piece of paper, making the words and letters fit the whole space. Do this in pencil, very faintly, just to give you an idea of how much space all the information will take up.

**6** Now you must decide on how to do the lettering, and practise it a little first.

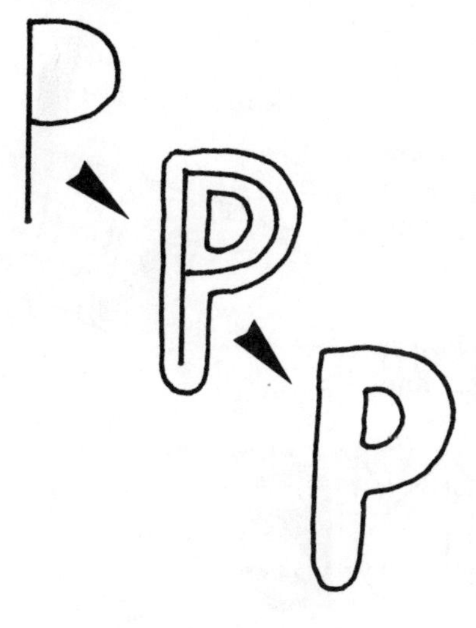


Here are some ideas:

*'Sausage' lettering*

Draw the normal shape of the letter very faintly. Now draw all round it, making the angles rounded. Rub out the first letter shape you drew. You can now colour the letter that is left, making it as bold and bright as possible. It is a good idea to outline the letter in black felt-tip pen later on.

Large 'sausage' letters take up quite a lot of room. Squeeze them together if you need to, hiding part of the second letter behind the first, like this:

When you put the letters together this way, outline the letters after they are coloured, or they will all merge into one, and will not be readable.

*Two pencil lettering*

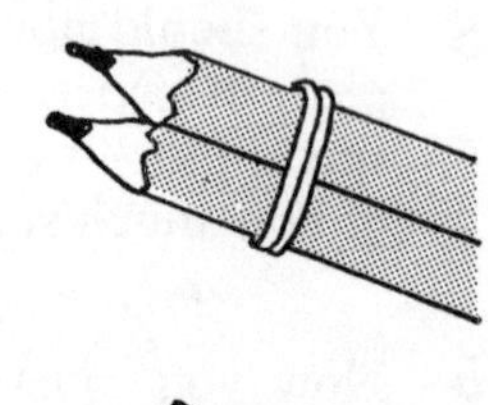

Fasten two pencils together with the elastic band so that the pencil points are level with each other.

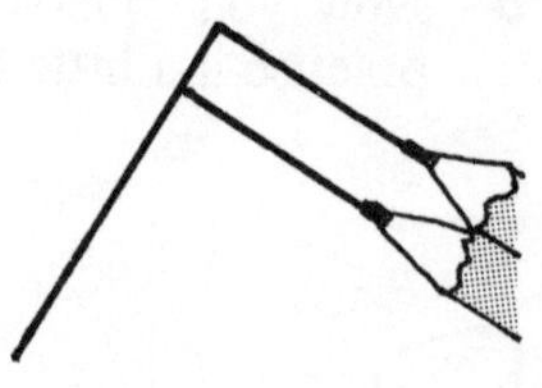

Holding the pencils at the angle shown, try to draw a 'pyramid' like this.

One side of the pyramid should have a very wide line, and the other should be very thin. Keep your pencils at the same angle *all the time* you are drawing out the other letters.

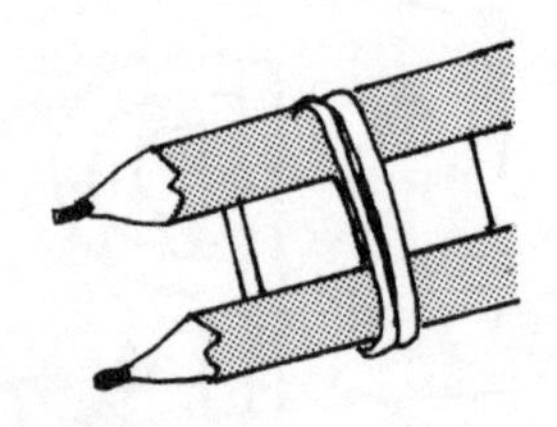

If you think the letters made by using the two pencils are too small, tie a rubber between the pencils to make them wider apart.

Draw in small lines to make the letters 'solid'. Colour in the letters, and outline them.

*Smaller letters*

Small letters, for less important parts of the poster, still need to be clear and readable. With a large felt-tip pen in a dark colour, practise making ordinary capitals even and well-spaced.

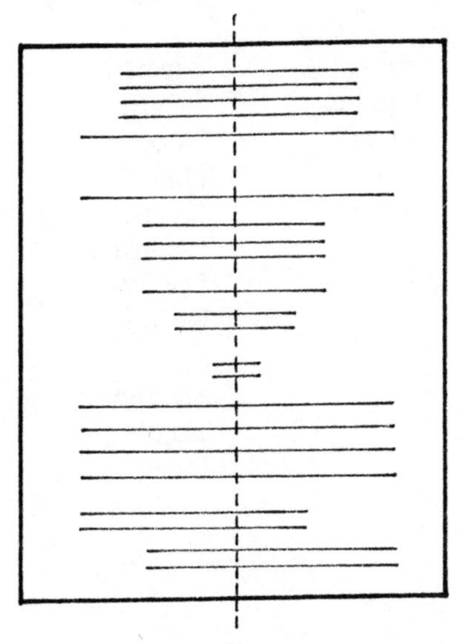

**7** You are now ready to carry out your lettering properly.

It is a good idea to rule a line down the centre of the paper; this helps you to see if the words and sentences are evenly spaced.

Now rule lines for the letters to sit on, *as well as* lines to show you where the tops of the letters are to come. Make these lines as faint as you can, so that you can rub them out later.

**8** Draw your lettering out in pencil, then colour it with felt-tip pens or poster paint. If you are going to outline the letters, wait until the next day before doing it. Even felt-tip pens take longer to dry than you think!

**9** Now look at your poster from one or two metres away and decide if any of it needs to be made clearer. Perhaps a decoration, a garland, or even a few ruled lines would add to its impact.

Ask where you may display it, then hang it up and wait for people to come to the event!

# THE CHURCH – A WORD PUZZLE

All the words below have something to do with the Church, and can be found somewhere in this book. The arrows give you a clue where to find them on the grid.

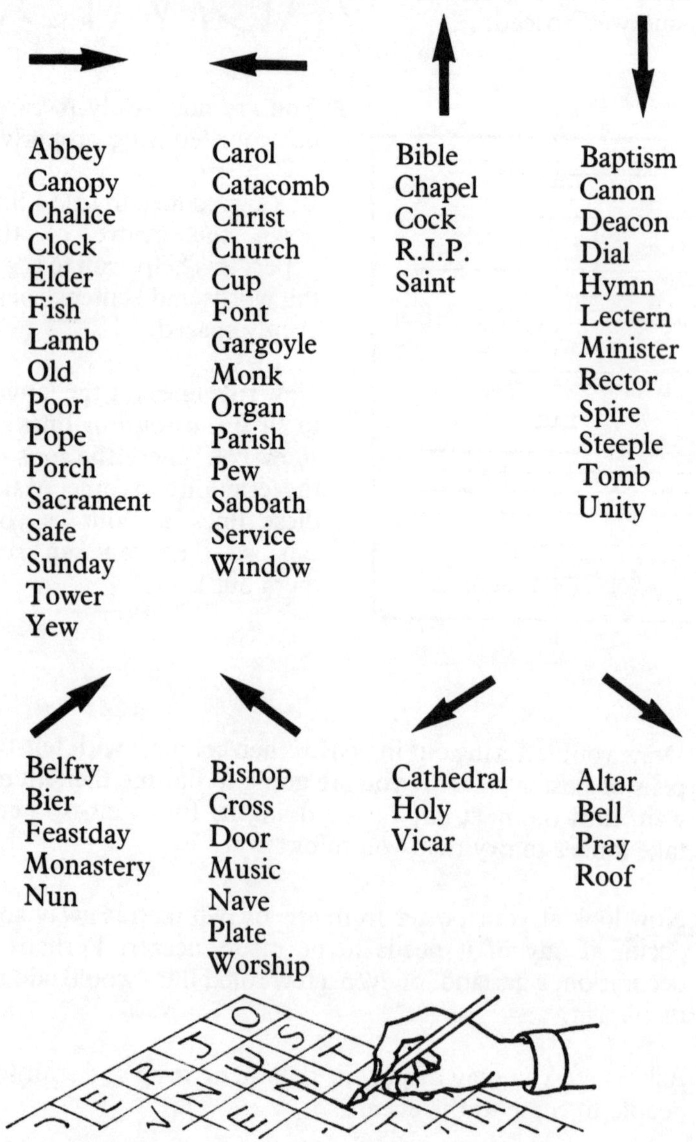

| → | ← | ↑ | ↓ |
|---|---|---|---|
| Abbey | Carol | Bible | Baptism |
| Canopy | Catacomb | Chapel | Canon |
| Chalice | Christ | Cock | Deacon |
| Clock | Church | R.I.P. | Dial |
| Elder | Cup | Saint | Hymn |
| Fish | Font | | Lectern |
| Lamb | Gargoyle | | Minister |
| Old | Monk | | Rector |
| Poor | Organ | | Spire |
| Pope | Parish | | Steeple |
| Porch | Pew | | Tomb |
| Sacrament | Sabbath | | Unity |
| Safe | Service | | |
| Sunday | Window | | |
| Tower | | | |
| Yew | | | |

| ↗ | ↖ | ↙ | ↘ |
|---|---|---|---|
| Belfry | Bishop | Cathedral | Altar |
| Bier | Cross | Holy | Bell |
| Feastday | Door | Vicar | Pray |
| Monastery | Music | | Roof |
| Nun | Nave | | |
| | Plate | | |
| | Worship | | |

| P | A | B | B | E | Y | S | E | L | Y | O | G | R | A | G | E | L | D | E | R | J | O |
|---|---|---|---|---|---|---|---|---|---|---|---|---|---|---|---|---|---|---|---|---|---|
| L | A | M | B | R | H | C | R | U | H | C | L | O | R | A | C | Y | E | W | N | U | S |
| T | N | O | F | S | U | N | D | A | Y | W | E | P | S | A | C | R | A | M | E | N | T |
| O | O | L | D | P | O | P | E | B | M | O | C | A | T | A | C | I | C | V | L | I | M |
| M | E | H | S | I | R | A | P | Y | N | B | T | H | E | X | K | N | O | M | E | T | I |
| B | P | O | O | R | E | A | R | T | O | W | E | R | E | T | C | A | N | O | P | Y | N |
| A | E | I | E | E | C | E | Y | N | S | D | R | L | P | P | O | R | C | H | A | D | I |
| P | L | I | H | R | T | C | V | I | R | S | N | C | L | O | C | K | U | D | H | I | S |
| T | B | T | C | S | O | A | I | A | J | U | O | V | E | H | H | Q | T | U | C | A | T |
| I | I | N | A | G | R | O | L | S | N | R | I | R | O | F | I | S | H | Q | U | L | E |
| S | B | N | N | R | E | O | D | P | U | C | O | L | C | H | A | L | I | C | E | T | R |
| M | O | W | O | D | N | I | W | I | A | M | Y | O | G | E | H | T | A | B | B | A | S |
| M | K | E | N | P | T | S | I | R | H | C | S | A | F | E | E | C | I | V | R | E | S |

Solution:

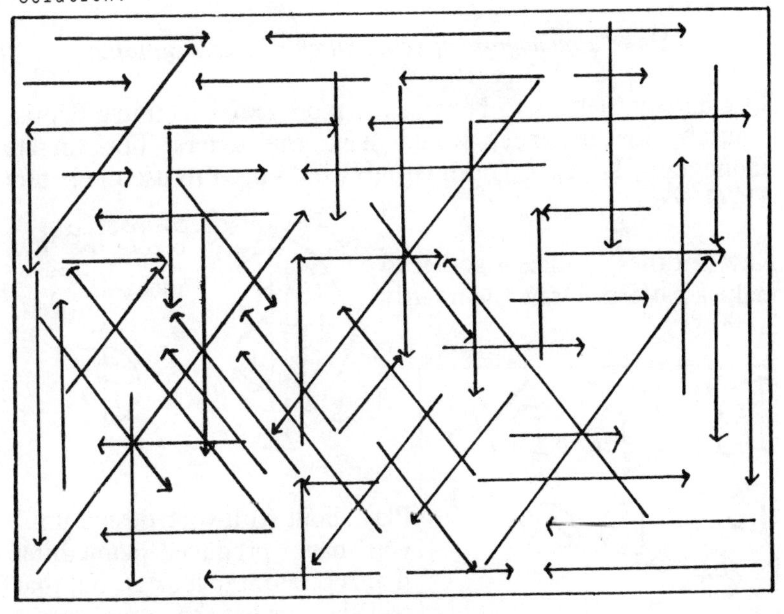

# MAKING A MONOGRAM

A monogram is made by putting two or three letters together to make one design. (*Mono=one*)

This is a monogram you will see in many churches. It is made up of the three letters IHS. (*See page 107 to find out what these letters stand for.*)

This monogram is a very old one, too, but is often used today as a badge Christians wear. (*See page 107.*)

*Make a monogram of your church or club's initials.*

Decide what letters to have in the monogram. Tetbury Baptist Church, for instance, would have the letters TBC in its monogram; Douglas Youth Group would need to use the letters DYG.

Now put these initials together to make a pattern. Draw them fairly large.

Or you could make the T into a cross, like this

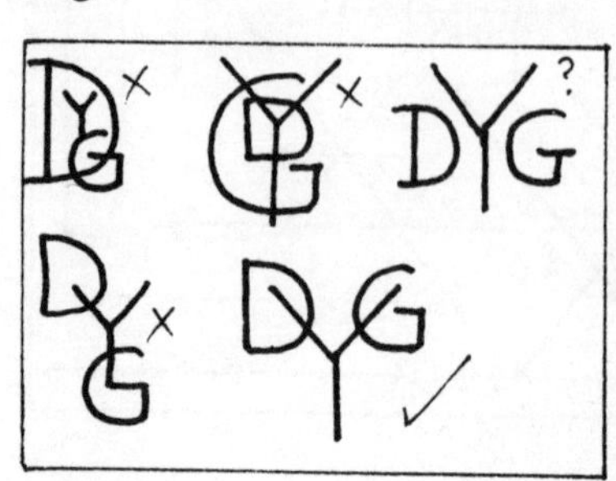


Play about with your design until you have produced something that is pleasant to look at, but that still shows what the letters are.

Draw out your chosen design large enough to be able to make the letters fairly solid, and fill them in with one colour.

Use any type of lettering, but see pages 113-115 for ideas on how to do it.

Perhaps someone will get the monogram printed onto notepaper, or on badges that can be worn, or even on sweatshirts! Show the design to your minister or leader, and talk over how it might be used.

# THE CHURCH AND MISSIONARY WORK

When the great explorers discovered new parts of the world, they not only expanded trade and communications, but took Christianity to people who had never heard of Christ. *Read Matthew 28.19 to see what command of Jesus they were fulfilling.*

These early expeditions led to missionaries going to all parts of the newly-found world. Some of these missionaries have names well-known to us now, like David Livingstone of Africa, William Carey of India, and Robert Morrison of China.

Christians want to share their faith and happiness in Christ — they simply cannot keep it to themselves!

**Dr Livingstone**

Mission work goes on at home, too. Sometimes Christians meet at street corners to sing and pray; others meet at huge open air gatherings to hear a preacher.

Christian pop songs are written and broadcast; there are speakers and singers on television; processions of witness parade through the streets, and thousands of leaflets, badges and posters are distributed to spread the Gospel of Jesus.

So missionaries do not necessarily go abroad to take the message of Christianity. Indeed, nowadays many missionaries come from other countries to ours, spreading the word here.

There are many missionary societies all over the world, of every denomination. Some missionaries are transported to remote villages by small planes; others walk the streets of big cities caring for outcasts, beggars and the sick. Some work in factories, or in the fields, some in the armed forces and prisons; some work in the shadows of the Himalayan mountains, others in hot deserts.

Perhaps one of the best known and best loved missionaries of our day is Mother Teresa, working with the deprived and miserable outcasts in India.

*Find out if your church supports a missionary society, and whether any of your church members is 'on active service for Christ' abroad.*

*And watch for signs of the quiet, almost unnoticed work of ordinary Christians spreading Christ's Gospel in your own town or village.*

# THE CHURCH IS A COMMUNITY

A community is a body of people, a fellowship, where everyone has something in common. A school is a community: each young person is there to receive education and to share activities within that school.

The Church is a community, too: a huge, world-wide one in its biggest sense. All Christians have something in common — following Christ — and they all share activities as Christians.

Your local church is a smaller community. Every person who attends shares something in common: they love, worship, and learn of God. They share in the activities that go on in that church.

Not everyone in a community is the same age. Your own family is a small community, and the newest baby is as much part of the family as is grandfather or great-grandmother.

So the church community is made up of people of different ages, from the youngest baby brought for baptism or dedication to the oldest member, who may even be housebound or in hospital.

Nearly all communities have leaders. Your town community may be led by a mayor, your school by a headteacher, your family by a parent, and the church by a vicar or minister.

## The church community

Just as there are different levels of education within a school, and probably several clubs for different ages and interests, so the church caters for all ages and interests.

Groups may specialise in educating children and young people in the church, but the adults are also learning. They listen to sermons or talks that young children would not be able to understand, and they have Bible study groups and church meetings that are suited to their age and responsibilities.

People within church communities, young and old, have different interests. Look at some of the activities some people do within the same church:

Mrs Lucy Barlow likes meeting people. After she has been to the church service, she goes to join friends in the church hall for coffee. She makes a point of looking out for visitors, and invites them along, too.

Mr David Craig is fond of music and has a good singing voice. He sings in the church choir, and goes to the choir practice every Friday.

Sheila Tomkins has just joined the Girls' Brigade. She is in the Explorers' Group. She likes the games and working for badges. She also meets her friends in 'Junior Church' on Sunday.

Old Mrs Brown lives on her own, but enjoys going along to her Women's Meeting on a Wednesday afternoon. She meets lots of people there, and always likes listening to the visiting speakers.

Mr and Mrs Jonathan Barker and their children have joined the church walking club. In summer they meet on Sunday afternoons to walk in the country. Families of all ages go too, and picnic together before going home.

Grandpa Cutts can't get out much on his own, but is taken to church by his neighbours each week. They also take him to the monthly 'Family Evening' so that he can join in the fun.

Mr and Mrs Frank Summers are interested in learning more about the Bible. Every week a small group of church members meet in their house. They read the Bible and discuss together what they have read.

Lisa Tostevin is 17. She belongs to the church Youth Club, which meets on Saturday nights to listen to records and play badminton. She also goes to their meetings after the Sunday evening service. There is usually a speaker or a discussion at these meetings.

What do the people in *your* church do?

*Find out what meetings, clubs, organisations or societies there are for people to go to.*

You know the members of your family community; think of your church as a family, and try to get to know *everybody*. Join in activities when you can; join a youth group or organisation, and get your friends interested, too.

# THE CHURCH IN THE COMMUNITY

The work of the Church does not stop after the church doors are shut on a Sunday. The Church is not a building, remember, but a body of Christians — men, women and children — who try to serve and follow Christ.

Every day of the week these people are living the Christian life, at home, at work, at school and at play. At their worship on Sundays they find the strength to go out into the world on Mondays and, in the name of Jesus, to meet others in all walks of life.

Christians get involved in all sorts of activities in their towns and villages. Some help in, or join, old people's or youth clubs; some belong to drama or choral societies, go to evening classes or sports clubs.

Wherever they go they show Christian friendship to the people they meet so that Christ's message of love and joy is seen and spread.

Many Christian people join in 'helping' activities, such as the Meals on Wheels service. There are many ways of helping, by visiting the old and the ill, by working for a hospital library, or in the Citizens' Advice Bureau, the St John Ambulance Brigade, the Samaritans, or a Good Neighbour Scheme.

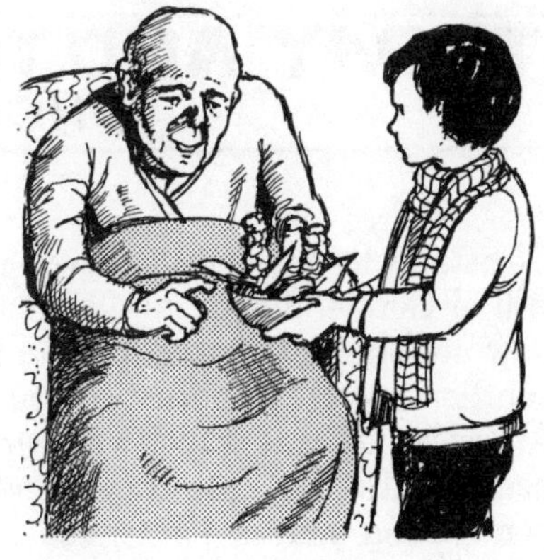

NSPCC

Lots of Christians do not confine themselves to the town or village where they live; they also support national societies, like the NSPCC which helps to prevent cruelty to children, or Christian Aid which sends supplies and teams of workers to help when there are disasters, famines, or desperate poverty anywhere in the world. Many other societies are supported as well: Save the Children, Mencap, War on Want, and Oxfam, for example.

Christians give money not only for their own ministers, and the repair and upkeep of their own church buildings, but for 'mission' to those less fortunate in their own country and other countries.

No one is too young, or too poor, to work for Christ on any day of the week. A kind word, a helping hand, or a friendly smile works for Jesus just as much as a thousand pounds sent to a charity. At home, at school and at play, you can show that you work for Christ and want others to come to know and love him.

# TODAY AND TOMORROW
## –THE CHURCH AT WORK

Christians have always believed that they should try to obey the will of God — that is, to do what God wants them to, no matter how unpopular this might make them. Sometimes this has led to conflicts with authority. From the Soviet Union to South American dictatorships, we hear stories of Christians who have had to suffer because they stood up for their faith. Sometimes persecution makes Christians realise how important faith is. Because *we* are allowed to go freely to church, we can take Christianity for granted.

Christ's work *will* go on; but it is never easy to count the numbers of people converted to Christianity in a single year, so *is* the Church growing? Perhaps we should simply ask, 'Is the Church growing *stronger*?' Large numbers of members do not always mean a strong church.

Christians are more united than ever before: Roman Catholic, Anglican and Nonconformist Christians meet and support each other. Christians are more tolerant of others, as they work and play with Muslims, Hindus, Sikhs and Jews. Religious leaders all over the world are becoming more involved with politics, putting Christian viewpoints across and working for peace.

We, the ordinary people, are important as Christians in the world today. We are not perfect, but with God's help we can break down barriers, work for peace, and take the Church of God into the future.

# USING YOUR
# AUTOFOCUS
# SLR SYSTEM

by Peter Lester

HOVE~FOUNTAIN BOOKS

**USING YOUR AUTOFOCUS SLR SYSTEM**

First Edition July 1988
By Peter Lester
Edited and Produced for Hove~Fountain Books by
Icon Publications Limited using Apple Macintosh™ and
PageMaker 2.0™ computer typesetting and design
Series Editor Dennis Laney
Editor & Designer David Kilpatrick
Printed in Great Britain by
Purnell Book Production Ltd

ISBN 0–86343–115–1

**Published by HOVE FOUNTAIN BOOKS**

45 The Broadway
Tolworth
Surrey KT6 7DW

34 Church Road
Hove
Sussex BN3 2GJ

UK Trade Distribution by
Fountain Press Ltd
45 The Broadway
Tolworth
Surrey KT6 7DW

# CONTENTS

# INTRODUCTION

When fully automatic cameras first began to reach a wide market, many experienced photographers refused to take them seriously, claiming that automation took all the craft out of photography. However, automation has quickly become an accepted part of camera design, and few of the people who were originally suspicious about automation have managed to resist the tempting attractions which modern 35mm compacts and single lens reflex cameras offer. Now almost all photographers, from the most successful professional to the complete beginner, can enjoy the exciting benefits of high-tech camera design, including the most important innovation in photography since automatic exposure – autofocus.

Autofocus has already revolutionized picture making with 35mm pocket cameras, but now there are an increasing number of SLR cameras available with this facility and they have become the ultimate picture taking machines. Just like all the other sophisticated features which today's cameras have to offer, autofocus simply exists to help you take better pictures.

Experts in photographic matters have often stated that if you are to be a successful photographer your camera should become an extension of your eye, and that there should be no technical obstructions between you and what you want to photograph. Now, automatic exposure, autofocus cameras can bring you as near as possible to this ideal, providing you with the ability to respond instantly to every type of picture opportunity without the obstacles caused by tricky technical operations.

On one level, automatic, autofocus SLR cameras can be used as easily and as quickly as a pocket camera. Conversely, many photographers use their autofocus SLR as an extremely practical and sophisticated tool, suitable for everything from sport and news subjects, to fashion and portraiture. Indeed, the true value of an AF SLR lies in the many levels at which it can be used and enjoyed. You don't outgrow a camera like this, you grow with it,using it to begin with as a means of taking successful high quality snapshots, and, as your skill and creativity begins to flourish, going on to use it as a means of making more expressive pictures. However, irrespective of what level you are at, whether you own an AF SLR already or are just considering buying one, we hope that this book will help you to understand and enjoy the very latest photographic technology, so that you can go on to make the kind of pictures that you like.

*– Peter Lester*

# 1: THE FULLY AUTOMATIC SLR

THE TOP of the range SLR cameras of today bear little resemblance to those little black boxes that many people grew up with. You are tapping into the very latest developments in micro-electronics when you take a picture with a bang-up-to-date SLR. They are packed with all kinds of sophisticated devices to make sure that your pictures are perfect, time after time, in even the most difficult circumstances or lighting situations.

To begin with,let's take a look at what sort of technical wizardry you can expect to find on today's advanced cameras. You might not find all the features mentioned here designed into every single AF SLR, but you will find at least a few of them on all models.

As any manufacturer, retailer or teacher connected with photography will tell you, unsharpness is the most common cause of a bad picture, and so this facility really does solve one of the chief problems experienced by photographers at all levels of experience, and the cause of a lot of disappointment and frustration.

Autofocus literally focuses the lens for you. You simply look through the camera's viewfinder, and point the lens at the subject, a tree in a landscape for example. You position the tree in the centre of the viewfinder, and when the camera tells you that the subject is in focus, usually through some form of sign in the viewfinder, you simply press the shutter release. The process of focusing takes a fraction of a second, usually far faster than you can react yourself, and you can be sure that the main element in your chosen view will always be sharp.

There are variations from maker to maker in the operation of autofocus and in the way it works, but fundamentally the above description holds true for all AF SLRs. There are also times when it doesn't work perfectly, which will be discussed later, but on the whole autofocus will provide you with sharp pictures in almost all circumstances if used properly.

## Exposure modes

A choice of exposure modes is available on most AF SLRs. Usually there are three; aperture priority, shutter priority and program. Occasionally they are referred to under slightly different names by some manufacturers, but in effect they perform similar functions. Some models claim to offer far more than three ways of exposing your film however. It might pay you to think about how many methods of exposure you might need to use before you pay the extra for all those permutations.

Fundamentally, all your exposures are determined by a combination of shutter speed and aperture size, chosen by you and/

# AN INTEGRATED PRODUCT

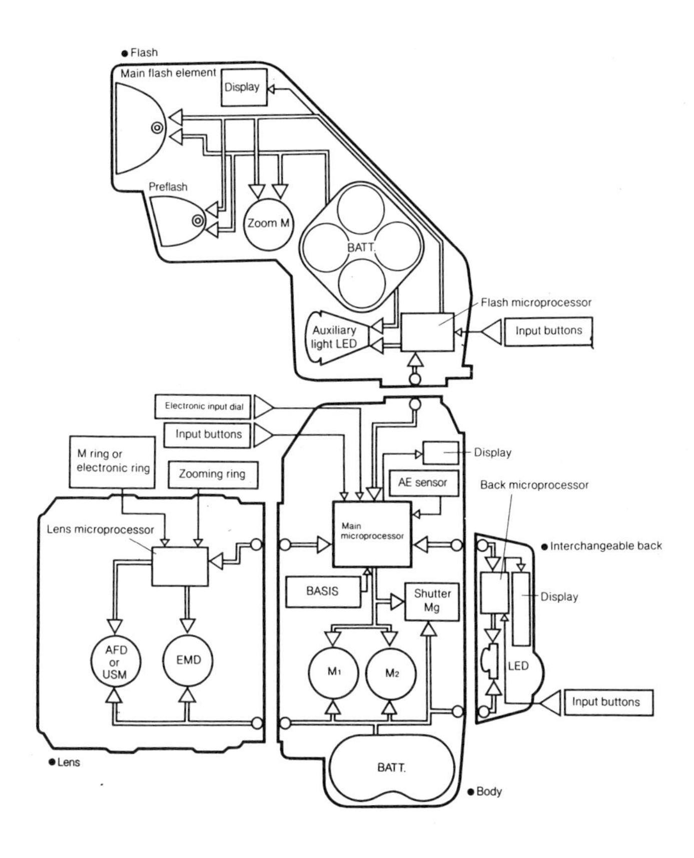


*This diagram of the operating logic of a Canon AF camera shows just how complex the design of photographic equipment has become – though the functions listed show equally well how easy such cameras are to use. In this model, the lens is linked not only to exposure systems but also to the flashgun which has its own zoom motor. The interchangeable back, like the flash, is an optional accessory and not built-in. Some AF SLRs include a simpler type of flashgun as part of the camera body itself.*

or the camera. The most common exposure mode on SLRs in the past has been aperture priority. This is often picked for general use, or when the size of the aperture you choose is of primary importance to the picture. When you switch to that mode, you simply choose the aperture you want, and the camera will automatically switch to the best shutter speed to go with it for a perfect exposure.

Shutter priority is chosen when the shutter speed is crucial to success. Again, simply switch to the right mode, choose a speed and the camera will choose the right aperture to go with it. We will look more closely at how the aperture and shutter speed affects the picture later on in the book.

The program mode is the easiest of all to use, as it actually chooses both aperture and shutter speed for you, usually a combination of the smallest aperture and the fastest shutter speed for any given lighting conditions. So with programmed exposure and AF you don't really have any technical operations to worry about, which leaves you free to concentrate on looking for good pictures.

However, many SLRs also have a fully manual mode, which allows you total control over which aperture and shutter speed you want to use should the circumstances require it. Some AF SLRs will also allow you to bypass the autofocus. One or two models actually change the program according to which lens, i.e. wide-angle, standard or telephoto, is in use, to allow for considerations of lens shake (a problem with longer lenses) to be taken into account.

## Interchangeable lenses

You can of course take excellent pictures these days with small compact 35mm cameras, indeed most of the technology now available in SLRs first appeared in these smaller types. However, compacts have a major drawback for those of us that have ambitions beyond being successful snapshooters.

Compacts are superbly convenient, and they provide consistently good results, but their use will always be limited as you can't fit them with inter-changeable lenses. There are now a few compacts with small,very short range zoom lenses built in, or a choice of two focal lengths, but they still can't compare with the full system of lenses that are available for even the humblest SLR.

Interchangeable lenses for SLRs snap in and out of the camera body quickly and easily with a single twist, offering a dramatic change of viewpoint without moving from the spot.

*Right: inside two popular AF SLR cameras – the complexity which makes matters simple.*

# INTERNAL COMPLEXITY

*This group of Olympus AF cameras and accessories shows a typical range of items available from one maker. The cameras include a model with a pop-up flash, and the lenses range from wide-angle and macro to zoom. The separate flash units are very much more powerful than any built-in flash, and in this photograph one is shown linked to the camera by an extension cable which permits angled lighting. All these cameras have built-in motor transport for the film; the rearmost model is shown fitted with a special data recording back. All the major SLR makers offer very similar products to these and the design of AF SLRs is in practice almost standardized.*

*Macro lenses enable the SLR user to record the subject life size or even larger on film – and very much larger on the print or projection screen. Photograph: David Kilpatrick.*

Lens systems offer you a tremendous range of picture-taking opportunities , enabling you to create sweeping landscapes, take in large groups or operate in small spaces such as your living room with a wide angle lens, while at the other end of the scale, you can use a telephoto to bring the action in close, and fill your viewfinder with the details you want.

There are also many specialized lenses, such as the macro type for close-ups, and a large number of zoom lenses which pack several useful focal lengths into one lens.

All SLRs have some form of sophisticated built-in light meter and some of the latest cameras have systems that work in milliseconds, measuring light as it falls on the film for complete accuracy. Many also offer some form of exposure compensation device, that can take into account either too much brightness or too much shadow in the scene, and adjust the normal reading accordingly.

Some of the more expensive models also provide a choice of metering patterns that allow you to take measurements from just one small portion of the subject, to ensure that the major element of interest in the picture is

*Above: built-in flash makes shots like this very easy to take naturally, without any fuss. Photograph by Chris Dickie. Right: fit a wide-angle lens, and the camera will program in extra depth of field.*

correctly exposed.

There is no need for anyone to feel overawed by flash any more. Most AF SLRs can make flash photography just as simple as daylight photography. Some SLRs now even have a small built-in flash unit which operates totally under the guidance of the camera's exposure systems, just as the larger accessory flash guns do when used in automatic mode. No need to work out complex calculations, the camera does it for you, even when using the flash bounced or as a fill-in.

Many of those mundane and often fiddly operations, such as film loading, winding on after each shot and rewinding at the end of the film, can now be taken care of automatically, so look for those features if you think that they are worthwhile. You'll find that you don't even need to set the ISO/ASA film speed when you load your camera, as even this task can now be performed automatically. A row of contacts in the film loading chamber of the camera read a code, now printed on all film cassettes, which contains all the necessary information about the film's speed and the number of frames on it, and automatically relay the data to the camera's electronic control systems.

# PROGRAMMED PERFORMANCE

## SPECIAL FEATURES AND EXTRAS

You will probably find a selection of the following features on almost any AF SLR, although the number of little luxuries on your chosen model will of course vary according to what you pay for the camera.

* Self-timer; ideal for those occasions when you want to include yourself in the picture, either on your own to give a sense of scale to a scene or to get in the picture with your friends or family. They are also handy for operating the shutter when a very slow speed is in use.

* Depth of field preview; a button or lever which will stop down the lens to allow you to see how much of your picture will be in focus with the aperture you or the camera has chosen. An extremely useful feature to have when shooting close-ups and other types of shots which demand critical attention to focus.

* Flash socket, a good idea if you are going to be using flash off the camera, such as in a studio. Some cameras only have a hot-shoe connector for flash, so check for the extra synch socket if you do intend to use the camera with studio flash.

All SLR cameras are simply the central items in a system of equipment which can be added to the camera to perform an extremely wide range of useful or specialized functions. Be sure that the system you choose contains everything you might possibly need for your future photography.

Items that you might like to add at a later date:

* Motor drive for advancing your film rapidly. Useful for sports or other action shots.

* Data back, a device which imprints all kinds of programmable information on the edge of each frame of film during exposure.

* Interchangeable focusing screens; there are many types available for advanced SLR systems including some useful for scientific or other specialized work.

The features and facilities mentioned above are all designed to enable you to take the type of pictures you like, and we will look more closely at how they can do that as we go along. If you are still only thinking of buying an AF SLR, check how many of the features are available on the models that you can afford and assess which offers the best value for money. Don't however, get carried away by all the marvellous technology. Remember that underneath all the glitz and glamour, a camera is still only a box for taking pictures.

# 2: ALL ABOUT AUTOFOCUS SLRs

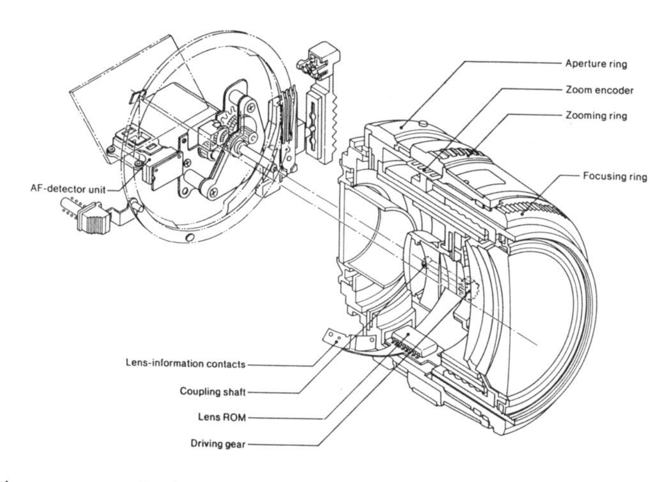


*The most popular form of AF system uses a motor in the camera body.*

CAMERA designers have developed AF systems in two distinct directions. One major manufacturer employs motorized lenses which receive information from an AF computer in the camera body, via electronic connections in the lens mount. All the other manufacturers, at time of writing, use a motor in the camera body, which powers the movement of the lens's internal gears by mechanical linkages in the lens bayonet mount.

Both systems have their supporters and critics. The lens system fans say that the mechanical linkages in the body-integral types are not as efficient as their electronic ones. The body-integral supporters point out that their system requires only one motor, while their opponents need a motor in each lens, which means extra weight and cost for a camera system.

Each system has its advantages and disadvantages. The majority of manufacturers do seem to favour the body-integral type, and there are great similarities between different makes – without any actual compatibility. In some cases a maker's new AF lens mount will allow you to use older non-AF lenses compatible with an earlier system, including independent lenses made by companies other than your camera's manufacturer. Check these details with the dealer before making your final choice if you already own an SLR outfit. Some AF systems do not include certain lenses, like extreme wide angles, which you may own.

## Focusing principles

On the face of it, a camera that won't let you take an out-of-focus picture seems nothing short of miraculous. Like most miracles there is a rational explanation behind it. Anyone who has ever used a rangefinder camera will have little trouble understanding how AF works. For those who have not seen a rangefinder, such as a Minolta CL or a Leica M4, these cameras work in the following way:

Two 'ghost' images of a small central portion of the composition are seen in the viewfinder. By turning the focusing ring these are gradually superimposed until they are exactly on top of each other and form a single image, at which point the picture is in focus.

Other rangefinders are similar in use to the little split image feature in the centre of most SLR viewfinders. You bring the two split parts together until they match up perfectly on either side of a dividing line, when the subject is then in sharp focus.

## Electronic versions

What happens in the case of AF SLRs is that the light forming the subject comes through the lens and is turned into two separate, but identical images by a type of 'beam-splitter' device. The two images of the subject fall onto sensors linked to the camera's computer, which assesses the different levels of contrast in the two image-patterns. The greater the difference between the two, the more out-of-focus the lens is.

The camera's 'brain' measures not only the difference, but also the apparent bias towards too distant or too close focusing, and transmits instructions for the AF motor to turn the focusing gear inside the lens accordingly.

While this is happening, the AF sensors continue to measure the contrast differences, with increasing accuracy as they are reduced. The final stage of focusing involves a few imperceptible steps of the motor to fine-tune the lens setting. All this happens in a split second,

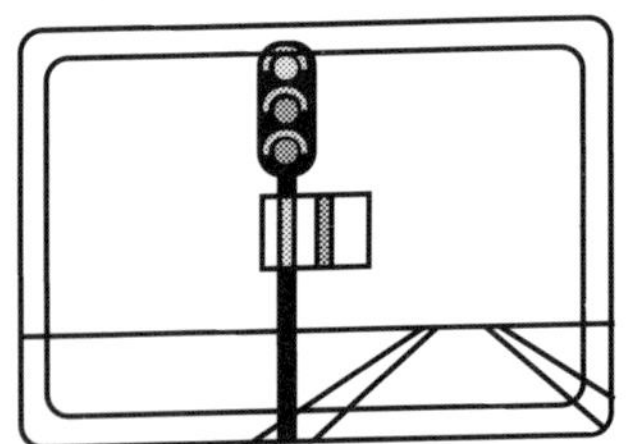

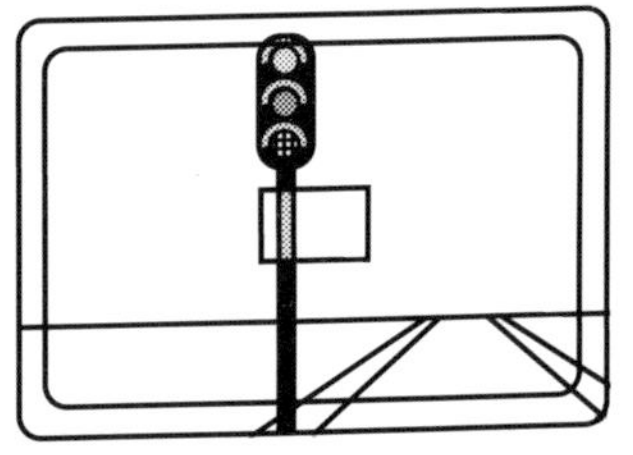

*The principle of the coincident-image rangefinder is not unlike AF focusing in its basic form (illustration from 'How to Use Your Compact Camera' by John Wade, also available in the Hove-Fountain Series).*

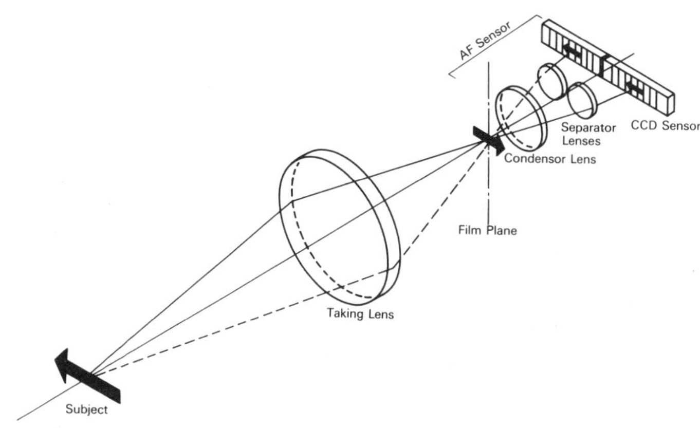


*The complex electronic and optical design of a modern SLR (top, courtesy Pentax) is based on a simple principle (diagram courtesy Yashica). The two sensor images are displaced when out of focus.*

*The effect of autofocus is immediate – it speeds up the reactions of the photographer by cutting out a process, or at least cutting it down to a minimum time. The photograph above was taken at 45cm.*

depending on how far out-of-focus the subject originally was and how far the lens elements have to be moved. On average a standard lens can be focused from its closest focusing distance (30-50cm) to infinity in well under half a second, and from 1 metre to infinity in less than 0.20 seconds. Try beating that manually!

There are of course slight variations in AF systems from manufacturer to manufacturer, but on the whole the principles are the same. As you can imagine,there are quite a few stages in the electronic processing of information inside the camera that I have left out for the sake of clarity. As we are primarily concerned with photography in this book, we won't spend pages and pages delving into the mysteries of ROM ICs, CPUs, DPUs, IPUs and CCDs.

## AF Modes

Now we have established that autofocus does have a simple rational explanation behind it, let's have a look at how to use it. There are two basic methods of using autofocus on many SLRs, single shot and continuous. Other peripheral focusing modes are available on one or two

*Less than a quarter of a second later, the same 50mm ƒ1.7 has switched to a precise middle-distance focus simply by moving the camera to change the composition.*

specific models, trap-focus for example. Continuous and single shot modes are called different names by different makers, but they all do more or less the same thing, as we shall see.

## Single Shot

This is the AF setting that you would use most of the time, and it is the most suitable one for static subjects such as views, buildings, family snapshots and portraits. Using this feature is as simple as using an exposure mode. In most cases your finger depresses the shutter release part way down to engage the AF system. While the finger is on the shutter release the lens will quickly focus to the distance of whatever is in the centre of the viewfinder and stay there.

To help you aim the AF system properly, there will usually be some sort of target area marked out in the centre of the viewfinder. When the camera has focused at the correctly assessed distance, a light confirming that the lens is in focus will flash on in the viewfinder. At this point, you simply depress the shutter release further to make the actual exposure.

If you decide that you don't

*Single shot mode is ideal for static subjects where continuous follow focus and motor drive are not needed (above). When the main subject is off-centre (left) use focus hold before adjusting the composition.*

want to make an exposure once the camera has focused on the subject, simply take your finger off the shutter button and choose something else to point at. You can do this as often as you like without shooting; just don't make that final pressure for the exposure. If you point the camera at something else without taking your finger off the shutter release, the AF system will stay locked onto the original distance.

Unless you make a mistake like this, using this system makes it almost impossible to take an out-of-focus picture. You simply can't depress the shutter button all the way down before the lens has been focused, but it is still up to you to make sure that the camera is focused on the right thing.

## Focus hold

Although a great number of pictures do have the main subject more or less in the centre of the frame, you will find that your creative instincts might demand that you try something different now and then. For example, you want to shoot someone looking out to sea, but they will be in a bottom corner of the picture and a vast expanse of ocean will fill the rest of the frame. As the sea will be in the centre of the shot, the AF system will ensure that it is sharp, with a strong possibility that the main figure will be out-of-focus.

The solution is very simple indeed. In the first place you would point the camera directly at the main subject, in this case the figure, so that it falls in the centre of the viewfinder, then touch the shutter release so that the camera becomes focused on the correct camera-to-subject distance. Keeping the finger on the shutter release so that the focus stays locked at that distance, alter the composition in the viewfinder until you have the shot that you want. At this point you can fire the shutter.

*The composition puts the subject off-centre*

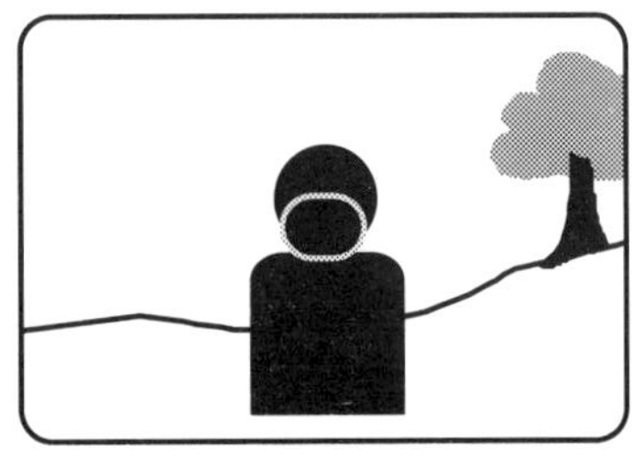

*Focus like this, hold, and re-compose*

*Most AF SLRs work in a way similar to AF compact cameras as far as Focus Hold or Lock functions go. First pressure on the shutter release activates the focusing; slight further pressure locks it, allowing free re-composition. In single shot mode models like the Minolta 7000 lock the focus as soon as the green light in the viewfinder confirms that the focus is correct; no further pressure is needed, and to re-focus you must remove your finger from the shutter release entirely. The graphics (right) are from John Wade's 'How to Use Your Compact Camera', another title in the Hove-Fountain Series.*

*When shooting two people or a group...*

*First focus on one only, then re-compose*

## Continuous mode

Unfortunately, not all subjects will oblige you by staying still while you shoot them. If you are trying to take a natural picture of the kids as they run around the garden, you will find your fingers jumping on and off the shutter release, constantly attempting to refocus. The continuous mode will do this for you. The first depression of the shutter release in this mode will cause whatever is at the centre of the viewfinder to become focused, as in the previous mode, but it will refocus constantly while you move the camera, or the subject moves in front of it. Consequently you can photograph sports, children and other lively subjects with ease.

However, bear in mind that you must keep the target in the centre of the viewfinder when you finally press the shutter release, as the distance of whatever is in the middle of the viewfinder at the moment of exposure will be the distance at which the lens focuses.

For example, if you are shooting a galloping horse as it moves from right to left across your path, you must keep it covered by the AF rectangle. If you let the horse slip away from the middle when you press for exposure, you will end up with nice sharp trees in the background, and the out-of-focus rear end of a horse disappearing out of the left side of the picture.

## Trap-focus

Not everyone can become an expert in 'panning' a shot in the aforementioned way, and also there are occasions when this method is not always suitable for stopping moving subjects. To cope with these problems, one manufacturer has come up with an ingenious system which will allow you to prefocus manually at the distance at which you have determined that the subject will appear. When the subject gets to that point, and the autofocus sensor detects a sharply-focused image, the camera automatically fires. Not everyone will need a facility like this, and only one manufacturer is offering it at the time of writing, but it might be worth investigation if you do a lot of wildlife or sports photography.

## Manual focus

Most AF SLRs also have a manual mode, because despite their ingenuity these marvellous machines do actually have to bow to human superiority in some circumstances – although not very many. Some AF lenses have a rudimentary focusing ring, while others employ other systems of movement, but whichever method your camera uses to allow you to focus the lens manually, you will probably find that it will still supply visible confirmation of focus in the viewfinder.

*For a photographer with a natural history bias like Peter Lester, continuous focusing is almost essential. Here he was able to track the moving targets and retain precise focusing until the right moment.*

*Trap focus could have been used by pre-setting on a fixed point just above the water. It would have caused the camera to fire as soon as the mother entered the focusing zone.*

## Problems

You will find some situations when your AF system will not work, and you will have to resort to manual focusing with sharpness confirmation in the viewfinder. Sometimes the light-level is too low or the subject has not enough detail. Under these circumstances, the focus confirmation will not work correctly either.

Autofocus needs a certain amount of contrast in the subject in order to work efficiently. In practice, the amount needed is not really that dramatic, so don't imagine that the system breaks down if you try to shoot anything that doesn't have the tonal contrast of a zebra. In an autofocus context, poor subject contrast means a scene with very close tonal values (a really foggy landscape for example) although very bright or very dark scenes may cause the same effect. In poor conditions, you may find that the lens will 'hunt' around looking for the right distance, but the focus confirmation light will not come on. A signal in the viewfinder will tell you to turn to manual or adopt another approach if you still want to take the picture.

Some of the newer AF SLRs will allow AF photography in quite dark conditions. Generally speaking, these employ an infra-red beam which can be bounced off the subject by a 'transmitter' in the camera body and this is 'read', as a substitute for normal light. This facility is primarily a part of the very sophisticated flash systems which are now appearing built into some of the newer SLRs; of which more later.

If the lack of contrast in your subject is simply due to a predominance of an evenly lit single colour in the scene, a black cat sitting on a black rug for example, then aim the camera at the nearest point to the subject – the edge of the rug perhaps – that contrasts with the main subject. You can lock the focus distance with the first press of the shutter release, recompose and shoot.

## Summary

The operation of your autofocus system might vary slightly from other types, but in principle they all do the same job with more or less the same degree of accuracy. You can rely on all AF systems to do a very good job of ensuring that your pictures stay sharp; indeed it is hard to persuade this type of camera to take an unsharp picture even if you want it to. However, you still have an important role to play in picture selection and composition. Take some time to investigate fully all the aspects of using AF, so that you can use them creatively for successful picture making.

# 3: HANDLING THE CAMERA

*The typical modern AF SLR is designed to fit the hand neatly – with a moulded grip at the right-hand end concealing the batteries which are essential to run an entirely electronic system.*

CAMERAS are attractive things, and it is easy to become seduced by the sleek look of the latest high-tech marvel. After making all the practical decisions about price and features, the deciding factor is often simply how the camera actually feels to you when it is in your hand. If you have used SLRs before, you will know that some of them slip into your hand and nestle there like a family pet, while others seem as enjoyable to hold as a lump of rock.

Every style and shape of camera will have its admirers and detractors, so the best policy is always to get your hands on as many cameras as you can before buying one, just to see which one feels the friendliest. After all, you wouldn't chance buying a pair of shoes without trying them on, and the camera needs to fit your hands just as a comfortable pair of shoes fit your feet.

## Holding the camera

AF SLRs might feel a little different if you are already used to operating an ordinary SLR, and you will probably hold it in slightly different way. Many AFs have a bulbous grip on one end, which doubles as a contoured surface for the hand to curl around, and often as a housing for batteries. Though AF SLRs have slightly different controls to the ordinary type, they are still held in the same way, that is with the base of the camera cradled in the palm of the left hand, with the thumb and forefinger extended to support the lens barrel, and the right hand cupped around the right side of the body with the index finger crooked over the shutter release.

Normally, the thumb and forefinger of the left hand would be used to twist the focusing ring of the lens. This isn't necessary with autofocus, so you can simply use the fingers as support for the lens. In some cases there are parts of the lens barrel which will move automatically during focusing, but these won't be affected by having your fingers touching the main barrel. If you are a hardened manual SLR user, you will just have to re-educate your fingers, rather like you have to retrain your feet if you begin to drive an automatic car after years of driving with a manual gear box.

The camera body should fit quite naturally into the right hand when you crook the index finger over the shutter release button: any other controls such as exposure modes, shutter speeds,aperture settings etc, should be operable with the fingers of either hand when the camera is held in this way. Try this before buying a camera, and then practice operating all the controls at home before going out to take pictures. Keep practising until you can work everything without taking your eye from the viewfinder.

## Familiarization

Top of the range cameras are smothered in features, functions and controls, many of which will be exclusive to a particular model, so always carry your manufacturer's instruction manual with you, and study it carefully, particularly before setting out to take pictures for the first time.

Make sure that you have the necessary batteries, fit them in and practise running through the controls. Experiment with the exposure modes and see what, if any, changes occur in the information that you will see in the viewfinder when you switch from mode to mode. If you do this while referring back to the manual, you'll soon begin to understand how and when to use the various features on the camera. The worst time to start finding out what it all means is when you are taking those once-in-a-lifetime pictures.

After checking through the various exposure modes, it is time to familiarize yourself with the autofocus system. As we saw in the previous chapter, there are one or two different types, each with its own capabilities. Some will focus on moving subjects,

# A RANGE OF DISPLAYS

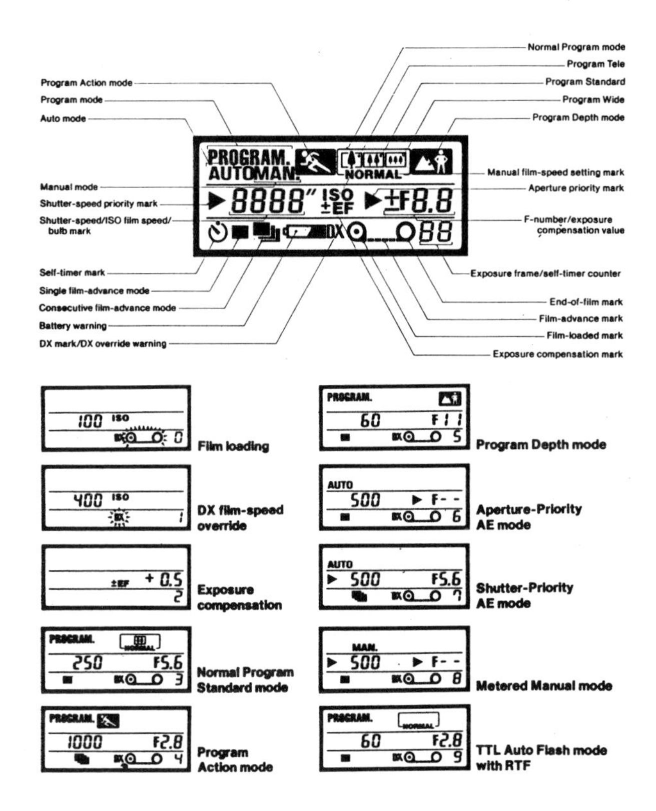


some won't allow you to take a picture unless the focus is confirmed, others will. Again, the answer is to practise – find out what if any the limitations of your system are. Simply point and shoot at anything and everything and don't forget the manual. Read, try it and check.

Once you know where all the knobs and switches are and what they do you can load a film. This is simplicity itself with most SLRs .

*Familiarization with the camera's modes is often a question of learning how to understand the display panel on the top plate and similar information seen through the viewfinder. These examples (courtesy Canon) show the many modes and functions available on one particular AF SLR in a simple graphic form, but a thorough study of the instruction manual helps the user interpret the display with the aid of this chart.*

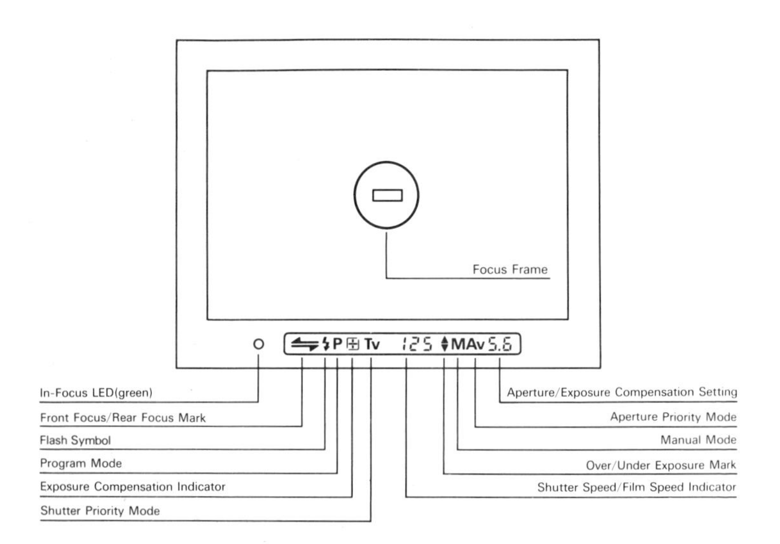


*A simplified set of icons and codes will normally be seen through the camera viewfinder, as above (courtesy of Yashica). There is not enough room for the full graphic displays used externally.*

## Film loading

As we have mentioned before, film speeds are almost always set automatically now, so you won't need to worry about them unless you want to use your film at a different speed from that recommended by the manufacturer. How and when to do this is explained in a later chapter. Many cameras have a small window in the back which allows you to see the cassette, providing a reminder, when you come to use the camera again, of which type and length of film is loaded.

Loading a film is not at all fiddly these days, as many cameras have a system which precludes the need for threading the film through a variety of spools. Loading is now often simply a matter of dropping the cassette into its chamber, pulling a length of leader across to a mark, and closing the camera back. When the back is closed, an automatic system grips the film and winds it on to the first frame. Again, not every camera has this feature, but a good proportion do. If you have problems with loading film quickly, an auto loading camera is well worth looking into; the instructions (right) show the loading sequence for this type.

# LOADING YOUR FIRST FILM

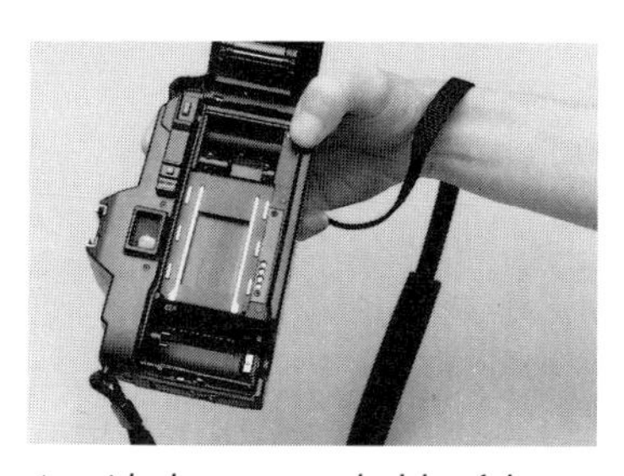

*1: with the camera held safely and the neckstrap out of the way, open the back fully and remove a plastic film-gate cover if present.*

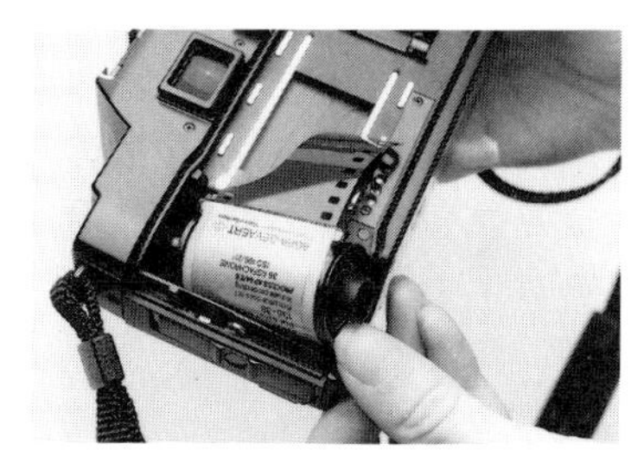

*2: insert the film cassette into the chamber as shown with the slotted end engaged to the rewind spindle and the knob downwards.*

*3: angle the cassette lip upwards a little and gently pull enough film out to reach the take-up spool or reference mark.*

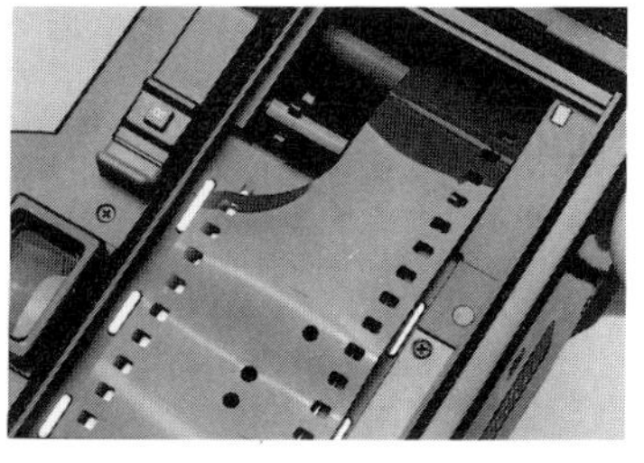

*4: place this leader of film flat over the sprocket drive gears, which should fit the perforations, and insert or place on take-up.*

*5: keeping thumb pressure lightly on the film at first, close the back firmly. At this point some cameras advance the film.*

*6: switch on camera to ensure film advance. Now check the LCD display to make sure the film is at frame 1.*

## Beating camera-shake

Familiarizing yourself with the controls of the camera is a quick and simple task, and it should only be a matter of minutes before you can take a successful picture by utilizing the camera's automatic facilities. However, because of all this automation photographers tend to forget their basic skills, such as supporting the camera properly during exposure. This is one task that has not been fully automated yet, and consequently poor handling is still the chief cause of ruined photographs.

Unsharp pictures are the commonest causes of disappointment for photographers of all levels. Autofocus was invented to help overcome this problem, but fuzzy pictures are not caused by poor focusing alone; they are also caused by camera shake – the chief symptom of poor handling.

By examining your pictures closely, you can easily tell if the fuzziness is caused by poor focus or poor handling. If there are any parts of the picture that are sharp – but they are the wrong ones – then you have a badly focused picture, which if you have an AF camera means you haven't read the instructions properly. If nothing in the picture is sharp, and in extreme cases straight edges seem to have a 'double vision' effect, then what you have is a picture blurred by shake.

This simply means that you have moved the camera during exposure, i.e. while the shutter was open. Even though your camera's shutter is only open for a fraction of a second, any movement of the camera during that time will record two or more slightly different views of the scene. There may be perhaps only a fraction of a millimetre difference in position, but that is enough to result in a blurred picture.

Try to remember that the effects of moving the camera during exposure vary according to which focal length lens is in use. Short lenses such as a 24mm wide angle, with an angle of view of around 85°, will show less evidence of camera shake than a long lens such as a 300mm which only has an 8° angle of view.

It is not, as some people imagine, the physical length of the lens that is critical in matters of camera shake; it is the degree of magnification. Don't be fooled into thinking that just because you have a very compact zoom or telephoto you can hold it steady at slower shutter speeds – it makes very little difference. You might be able to hold small lenses a little more securely, but even a very small sized telephoto lens really does need to be held with great care if blur is to be avoided.

The rule of thumb is never to use a lens at a shutter speed slower than the nearest numerical equivalent to its focal length. For

# FOCUS BLUR vs. CAMERA SHAKE

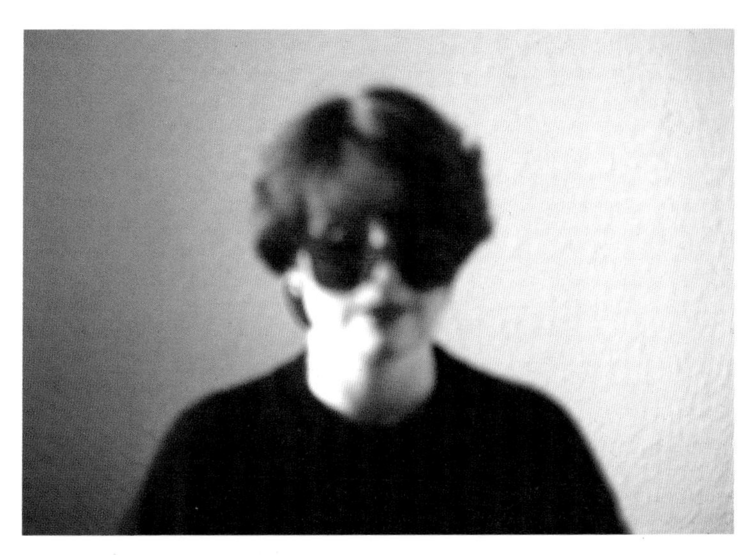

*It is easy to tell the difference between focusing blur (top) and camera shake (bottom) by looking at the way that the detail is blurred; soft edges reveal focus error, double images camera shake.*

*For the top photograph David Kilpatrick used a 17mm lens – and was able to hand-hold at 1/30 with sharp results. The 500mm mirror lens shot below needed 1/500 to stand a chance of being sharp.*

example, if you are using a 50mm lens, then never use a shutter speed slower than 1/60 second. There usually isn't a 1/50 shutter speed on modern cameras, so 1/60 is chosen because it is the nearest. If you have a 200mm zoom lens, then never use a speed slower than 1/250 at the 'long end', or if you are shooting with a 28mm wide angle go no slower than 1/30.

Don't forget that this is only a rough guide. Everyone will have their own limitations, but the correct stance and skill in holding the camera are certainly worth developing. You might turn out to have a genuine talent for photography, but nobody will appreciate your skills if the pictures are always fuzzy.

Irrespective of which exposure mode you use, the shutter speed that either you or the camera has chosen should be displayed somewhere in the viewfinder or on top of the camera, either as an LED or a liquid crystal display. Keep a check on what this display is telling you and make sure that the shutter speed chosen will be suitable for a sharp picture with the lens you have fitted. Some of the more sophisticated cameras actually do this for you. They have a program mode which bases its choice of shutter speed and aperture on the focal length of lens in use, thus ensuring that there is less likelihood of your picture being ruined by camera shake.

## Use a tripod

When the information in the viewfinder or elsewhere makes it clear that a slow shutter speed will result from the exposure you are about to make, and changing modes or focal length is not a suitable solution, you must look for additional support. This may be from something around you such as a wall, a tree or the car, but best of all, use a tripod. Tripods are viewed by many as cumbersome, annoying items to have to carry around, but they are sometimes the only safe bet for a good picture.

Films rated at ISO 100 and

*A good tripod is important, and should be portable but substantial enough to support tele lenses.*

*Once you have a tripod, you longest shutter speed becomes infinite – it's only limited by how long the batteries last. Night-time shots with streaks from car lights are easily tackled. Photograph by Walter Taylor.*

below quite often result in slow shutter speeds, even at quite wide apertures, in anything less than bright sunlight. So if you use a zoom lens regularly as many people now do, you will find that pictures taken at the long end might well end up fuzzy. To try to avoid slow shutter speeds you can always use a faster film, ISO 400 for example, and you may then never need a tripod in average daylight. However, although faster films are of extremely good quality these days, they are not as crisp and colourful as slower emulsions, so do think about taking a tripod or even a monopod.

## Carrying cases

If you are simply going to use the camera with a standard lens and no accessories, then you can simply carry it around on the neck-strap, either inside an ever-ready case or without any covering apart from the lens cap. However, if you want to take along a lens or two and a few accessories, then it might be best to buy a custom designed gadget-bag. Gadget-bags go through frequent stylistic changes, but what you should always take into account when choosing one is ease of access, lightness (photographic equipment is heavy

*A tripod also opens up worlds of experiment. Here, Peter Lester needed a long exposure under woodland cover with a special infra-red film to obtain unusual colours.*

enough without adding to it) and protective strength.

Aluminium cases are strong and useful for storing equipment, but for practical everyday photography they are useless. You have to put them down to open them for access to your equipment; they are bulky, heavy and quite capable of inflicting bruises, scratches and dints when you are carrying them. As for soft cases, the latest design with a mile of zip and a plethora of pockets might look very smart and businesslike, but are you sure you can you find your lens hood or a filter quickly in all those pockets? Choose the smallest bag you can for practical purposes, with a good wide opening at the top to allow you to get hold of what you want, when you want it.

Look for plenty of padding and adequate compartments inside to stop your lenses and camera banging together, and just a couple of pockets for filters and extra film. The more pockets you have, the more junk you will invent to put in them, thus weighing yourself down needlessly. Finally, choose a bag with a broad carrying strap, that has a non-slip surface, so that the bag doesn't cut off the circulation to your arm, and so you don't have to make frequent grabs for it as it heads for the floor.

As an alternative to the large carry-all type of bag, many photographers are now choosing carrying pouches. This type of bag, often called a snout-case, is worn on a belt around the waist, and allows you to carry an SLR with a mid-range zoom lens, film and perhaps a small flash in a front pocket in comfort. You use it rather like a gun holster, and if you only use a single zoom lens as many people do this could be the ideal safe and comfortable means of carrying your camera.

---

## SHOOTING POSITIONS

• Think of yourself as a frame for firmly supporting the camera.

• Hold the camera securely with the palms of the hands in firm contact with the camera body.

• Don't hold the camera with just the fingers, let it sit in the hands.

• Don't wave your arms around like a pair of wings, keep your elbows tucked right into your abdomen, to form a bracket on which the weight of the camera can rest.

• Keep your legs apart and rest your weight evenly on both feet. If you are on tip toe, or balanced on one leg, you will not be offering a firm support.

• Breath out slowly and press the shutter gently, don't stab it, at the point just before you take in a breath.

*When a very slow shutter speed seems unavoidable, try one of the following dodges*

• Sit the camera on a wall, compose the scene as best you can through the viewfinder and use the self-timer if you have one.

• Jam the camera up against a wall, a tree or some other static object.

If the shutter speed is just a little slower than you would prefer, try shooting from one of these positions.

• Sit on the ground with your legs bent up in front of you. Put your elbows on your knees.

• Lie face down with your weight on your elbows.

• Kneel on one knee and support your elbows on the other.

• Lean against something firm.

# 4: EXPOSURE METERING

*Auto exposure has many advantages. Could you work out the correct settings for this picture quickly enough to shoot it? With an AF auto exposure SLR, you simple point and shoot.*

ALL THE electronic functions to be found in an AF SLR obviously need a lot of power, but how much, and what kind? Alkaline batteries are the best. They cost a little bit more to begin with but they could work out cheaper in the long run. You will get through a set of these every 30 films or so in one of the more advanced models without any accessories in use. Ordinary zinc carbon types will only do about 10 in the same circumstances, while rechargeable nickel cadmium batteries will service about 15 or more.

Batteries are affected by extremes of heat and cold, but in normal seasonal conditions you shouldn't experience any problems with them. However, if you are going to leave the camera unused for long periods, it is always advisable to remove batteries from the camera, just as it is with any other battery-powered item.

## Metering Limitations

Automatic exposure was as much a photographic revolution in its day as autofocus is now, and the two features combined certainly make photography easy and fairly foolproof. Autofocus SLRs usually come with a choice of exposure

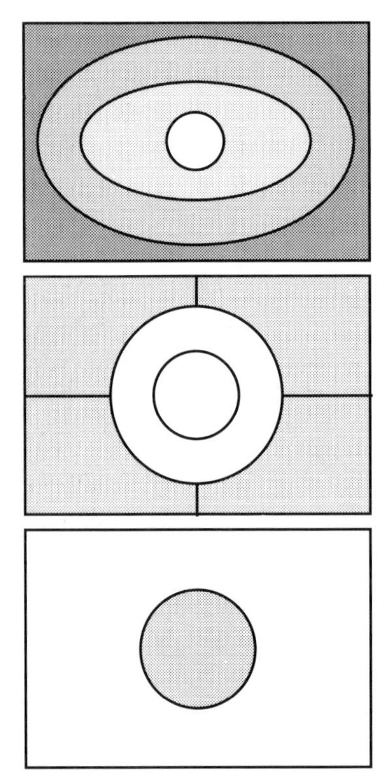

*Exposure metering in SLRs often uses a simple centre-weighted averaging pattern (top) where the sensitivity of the meter increases towards the centre of the scene. In 'intelligent' systems like the Canon EOS an evaluative pattern (middle) is used with computer comparison of the divided subject areas to recognise bright skies. A semi-spot or partial metering pattern (bottom) always bases the exposure on the centre area only. All work equally well with a typical sunny-day shot (right).*

modes, each of which is designed to provide you with a different method of making an exposure of the scene before you.

We will look at several types of metering systems and the modes that you might use, each providing a different way to exposing film to suit a range of subjects and conditions. At the heart of any exposure system is a metering cell to measure the light coming from the subject into the camera and to provide information, either to you or directly to the camera for an average exposure calculation.

There will, of course, usually be a range of tones in a scene, but the meter scrambles these to arrive at an average on which it bases its recommended combination of aperture and shutter speed. Unfortunately, sometimes there will be an extremely wide range of tones in the scene, especially if you are shooting on a bright, sunny day. An exposure based on the average of these tones would cause the brightest area of the scene to be overexposed and the darkest underexposed.

The important thing to remember is that film has its limitations, and metering systems are designed to deal with average conditions. The human eye can distinguish detail in deep shadows and then adjust to bright areas and see detail in that too; unfortunately, film cannot. This is why the most up to date AF SLRs

*With a subject backlit by a single spotlight, average metering would yield much too light a result; spot metering from the fully lit skin tone gives a perfect exposure. Photograph by David Kilpatrick.*

have such a variety of features, they are simply there to help you fine-tune your exposures to suit every type of exposure situation and difficult subject matter, within the limitations of film.

## Patterns

As the majority of photographic subjects are composed so as to occupy the centre of the viewfinder, manufacturers arrange the metering cells to read from this area. This is referred to as centre-weighted metering and is the most common type.

Many of the latest cameras, especially AF types, have very sophisticated metering patterns, and many offer a choice of two or more to select. Many metering systems now read from three to six points on the overall field of view to provide a truly average exposure, and one or two can even deal with problem lighting automatically by estimating subject contrast.

For example, one of the more advanced systems can assess if a scene is strongly backlit and adjust the exposure to compensate, thus avoiding a silhouette being made of the main subject.

As well as average metering, many AF SLRs commonly have spot metering. You can aim a spot meter at a very specific small area of a scene, rather as you would point the AF target in the middle of the viewfinder. The area which is covered by the spot meter is usually indicated in the centre of the viewfinder, but you don't have to restrict its use to the centre of the scene.

You can pick any small area in the scene to which you want to give exposure priority. Take a reading with the spot meter, lock the exposure using the AE lock that you will almost certainly find on an AF SLR with spot metering, and then reposition the subject in the viewfinder into a suitable composition. Once you have mastered this technique, you can use the spot meter for all kinds of tricky lighting conditions, particularly backlit portraits.

## Compensation

Some scenes will fool even the smartest exposure systems. The legendary black cat in the coal cellar will (thanks to the average metering system) be rendered a grey cat in a slate cellar, and a virgin white snow-scene will suffer a similar fate by also being rendered grey. In both of these situations you have to fool the meter even further by making it increase exposure for the light scenes and decrease it for the dark.

You can adjust exposure in several ways. You can be crafty yourself, or you can let the camera do it for you. The experienced photographer will probably switch to manual if the camera allows it, and adjust the

*Subjects with even lighting but light or dark tones need compensation, as these two pictures by Peter Lester show. The white flower needed one stop more exposure (+1) and the slate rock 1/2 stop less (-0.5).*

shutter or aperture to provide an exposure one or two stops more, or less, than the one suggested by the meter. Alternatively, you might simply bracket your exposures by taking one or more shots with more and less exposure on each side of the one recommended by the meter. Some cameras even have a system which will bracket exposures automatically, so you might never need to bother with manual.

With most cameras you have an exposure compensations switch or dial to give plus or minus a stop or two, or failing that you can trick the camera by increasing or decreasing the film speed setting, or use the backlight button. At least one manufacturer now provides a highlight and shadow bias setting on the metering system. This will compensate for either very bright toned or very dark scenes, and renders their correct tonal values – really black cats in properly sooty coal cellars, and sparkling white snow scenes or wedding dresses.

AF SLRs have a terrific range of exposure systems, although some, like the highlight and shadow bias, are unique to specific cameras. All these facilities are simply there to help with tricky light, and they will all have more or less the same effect, but don't forget that in most cases it is still up to you to make the decision to use them.

## Exposure modes

Modes are the different ways in which you can combine the size of lens aperture and the speed of the shutter to cope with a range of subjects and conditions, and to allow you total control over the way in which you depict a scene. There are four basic modes, which are called a variety of fancy names by various manufacturers in order make them sound different. These are aperture priority, shutter priority, programmed and manual.

It is a very strong temptation to leave the camera to do all the thinking by setting the program mode and forgetting all about creativity. Indeed this is probably not a bad idea when you first start to use an AF SLR. As time goes by and you get more confident with all the features that you have to play with, the urge to experiment will probably be too great for you to resist. This is the time to start enjoying the benefits of the other exposure modes.

The aperture is an adjustable hole inside the lens which controls how much light is allowed through. The size of the aperture is denoted by *f*-numbers which you will see on the lens barrel and displayed, along with other exposure information, somewhere in the viewfinder or as a liquid crystal display on top of the camera. Exposures are calculated by balancing the chosen size of the aperture with the amount of time you have the shutter open. You can make the same exposure, i.e. let the same amount of light through to the film, by a whole range of aperture/shutter speed combinations. For example; a correct exposure of *f*5.6 at 1/60 will allow through the same quantity of light, and provide exactly the same amount of exposure as *f*8 at 1/30, *f*4 at 1/125 or *f*3.5 at 1/250.

However, the size of the aperture and the shutter speed have other important bearings on the picture, apart from simply controlling the amount of light let onto the film. This why you are offered a choice of aperture or shutter priority.

## Aperture priority

The aperture chosen affects what is known as the depth of field, which is simply the distance in front of and behind the main subject that objects will also appear in sharp focus. The larger the aperture you choose, the less depth of field you have to play with, and consequently the more careful you must be in choosing what to focus on. Autofocus cameras will obviously ensure that the small area covered by the

*Identical exposures from different modes – top left, manual (1/125 at f8); top right, aperture priority (1/60, f11); bottom left, shutter priority (1/1000, f2.8); bottom right, program (1/350, f4.5).*

AF target is sharp, but if you want all the foreground and background to be sharp too, then you have to choose an aperture that will give you this result.

For everyday subjects aperture priority is the one favoured by most photographers, as the choice of what to have in or out of focus is very often the major creative decision when composing a picture. When this mode is chosen, you simply pick the aperture that suits the shot you are setting up, the camera will then choose the fastest shutter speed available to give you a good average exposure. In some cases you might have chosen a very small aperture which will result in a fairly slow shutter speed, too slow for you to hold the camera still enough to avoid camera shake. In this case the camera will probably warn you, at which point you will simply have to choose a larger aperture, use a tripod or perhaps even flash.

The choice of a small or large aperture is certainly not an arbitrary one. As we shall see in a later chapter, the size of aperture can affect your picture dramatically. When you choose an aperture, you also choose whether to have everything in sharp focus from the camera to the horizon, or to selectively focus on one object, allowing the background and foreground to blur in contrast. Examine the shots on page 49 carefully!

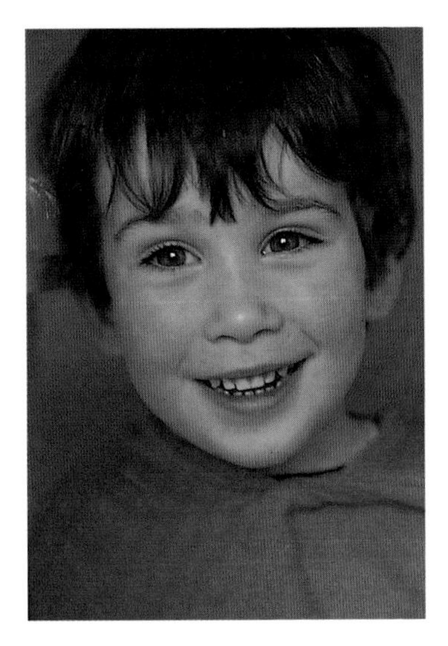

*Above: for a simple snap like this happy portrait by Chris Dickie, programmed exposure is perfect.*

## Shutter priority

With this mode chosen, you simply select the shutter speed you want, and the camera will give you the smallest aperture available for an average exposure. Broadly speaking, if stopping action is your priority, then the shutter speed will be your first consideration, so this mode may be what you would use for sports, wildlife and other action subjects.

As with the aperture, shutter speeds can be used to create pictorial effects such as blur or to freeze motion, especially with some of the better models with speeds up to 1/4000 second.

# DEPTH AND FROZEN ACTION

*Depth of field from the gate to the church meant stopping right to ƒ16 on aperture priority, top; anticipating passing runners meant leaving the camera on 1/500 and shutter priority, bottom.*

## Program mode

This is often called snapshot mode, because it allows you to simply to point and shoot. You don't have to choose the aperture or the shutter speed, the camera chooses both according to circumstances. For most average scenes, the camera's computer memory will choose the fastest shutter speed and smallest aperture combination it can for the available lighting conditions. The term snapshot really does not do the average program mode justice. On AF SLR's, they are really quite complex and sophisticated features.

On page 49, the exposure data for the comparison shots between four modes show an unusual setting – 1/350 at *f*4.5. This is because all program modes adjust the aperture and shutter simultaneously, and the better types do so in half-step stages which means they can be accurate to within 1/4 of an *f*-stop. The progression with this camera runs 1/250 at *f*4, 1/350 at *f*4, 1/350 at *f*4.5, 1/500 at *f*4.5, 1/500 at *f*5.6 and so on.

One or two manufacturers have programs that detect which lens is in use and adjust the bias towards either the shutter speed or the aperture that will ensure the best average exposures for either wide angle (aperture bias) or telephoto (shutter bias) shots. If a zoom lens is in use, the program will also change according to which focal length is in use. Some programs will let you shift from combination to combination manually, as the subject or lighting conditions change, or to adapt to your changing ideas. So, although programme modes do offer very simple photography, they are by no means simplistic features, in fact they could be described as becoming increasingly 'intelligent' feature. They can provide far more consistent results than the average photographer can manually.

## Summary

The principal function of your exposure modes is to provide you with a good average range of tones, depicting the scene that you have chosen to photograph. However, these sophisticated systems offer much more than that; they offer total control over every type of light, every type of subject and every type of tricky combination of the two. Despite its apparent sophistication, however, the camera still can't do everything for you; it still needs you to tell it what to do sometimes. So be prepared to assess the scene before you leave it up to the camera. Think about how the many exposure functions on your particular model can assist you to make a great picture, rather than simply relying on program mode to make an average one for you.

# 5: LENSES

*Above: a typical range of lenses for one AF system (Pentax) includes several different zooms, standard and telephoto lenses. The white finish often indicates a telephoto with a special optical quality.*

A MAJOR part of the craft of photography is the creative use of different focal length lenses. The facility of interchangeable lenses is what makes the SLR camera, AF or otherwise, the most flexible photographic tool available. To ignore the advantages that all those different focal lengths can offer is to squander your most important photographic resource.

With the range of AF lenses available, you can shoot vast, sweeping panoramas with a wide angle, or pick out an interesting distant face in the crowd with a telephoto. Fit a zoom and you can do both without moving from the spot. By choosing the right lens you can photograph anything from the very smallest to the very largest objects, from close to or from far away. Get to know what your lenses can do for you, they really are your flexible friends.

Autofocus systems do not, as yet, generally offer as many lenses as ordinary SLR systems do, but there are enough different focal lengths available to keep even the most adventurous photographer happy. AF lenses do differ somewhat in appearance from ordinary optics; the most important differences lie in their mounts and internal workings.

As we explained earlier, one system of autofocus operates by

*The new generation of AF lenses is very sharp – and AF helps even the inexperienced photographer focus on fine details to create memorable images with high quality, capable of considerable enlargement.*

*This slide by Peter Lester shows highly selective focusing using a wide aperture to blur the background and emphasize the main subject; subtle back-lighting adds to the effect.*

*To allow the use of older (Yashica-Contax mount) lenses on new AF models, Yashica offer a 1.6X converter which gives AF operation. It turns an older 50mm into an 80mm AF – with limited functions.*

including a motor in each lens, which is fed information, via electronic couplings in the mount, from a computer in the camera body. This allows very rapid transfer of information and each lens can have a motor specially designed for it.

Body-integral AF systems have mechanical linkages between the motor inside the camera body and the lens – one motor to drive every lens in the system. Each system has its advantages and disadvantages, and it is up to the user to decide which to buy. More important may be the question of lenses you already own and do not want to lose.

## Compatibility

Normally when a manufacturer introduces a new model of camera, the lenses from the superseded body are wholly compatible. In the case of AF, this is not always true. There are so many differences between AF lenses and ordinary lenses that some companies did not attempt to design the new mounts to be compatible with the old. For people who had invested a good deal of money in a lens system for their old body, this was quite a blow. However, some manufacturers have managed to design a new mount for their AF

*Some converters adapt old system lenses (such as Minolta MD) to new AF camera bodies – without AF, and with a small increase in focal length such as 1.2X. The normal result (top) becomes as shown below.*

SLRs which will also allow the use of some lenses from the old systems. In some cases, the older lenses can be used on the new mounts with the addition of an adapter to give full AF functions, while others can be used on the new cameras in manual mode only, but with the advantage of focus confirmation in the viewfinder.

One of the advantages of the older manual focus cameras was the huge range of moderately priced independent lenses available for them. Camera manufacturer's own brand lenses are usually very good, but are often quite expensive. Independent specialist lens makers were able to produce inexpensive manual focus lenses for use on a variety of famous brand bodies, but so far the scope for repeating this operation in the AF market has been limited by various patent restrictions.

This means that in most cases lenses can only be made under licence, with the result that so far only a very small number of independent AF lenses are available. At time of writing, AF prices are a good deal higher than they are for manual focus lenses due to the lack of competition. However, this situation will probably not last indefinitely and licences have been given to some independent makers to use the microchips found in 'genuine' lenses – already the choice is widening monthly.

## Focal Length

As you probably know already, lenses come in different sizes, known as focal lengths. The focal length of a lens is the distance from the optical centre of the lens to the film plane and it is expressed in millimetres, e.g. 50mm. The shorter focal length lenses, i.e. 35mm down to 21mm, are usually called wide angle lenses; 50/55mm lenses are standards, and 90mm – 300mm plus are telephotos.

The focal length of the lens dictates its angle of view – how much of the scene before you it will take in. The human eye has an angle of view, or field of vision if you like, of about 70-80°, although we tend to concentrate on a narrower area than that. A 50mm standard lens has an angle of view of 45°, which is closer to the visual area that we concentrate on, and so is accepted by most photographers as the lens which provides a picture closely resembling natural vision. A 21mm wide angle takes in over 85°, while a telephoto of 200mm focal length takes in only about 12°, which means that these lenses have a much wider or narrower view of the world than our normal vision.

The degree of magnification, i.e. how much larger or smaller than real life an object will appear in the viewfinder, also changes in direct proportion to a lens's angle of view and focal

*The top photograph was taken with a standard 50mm lens. The bottom one was taken with a 28-135mm lens set at 28mm, and the central frame shows how much would have been included at 135mm.*

*Above: perspective is a function of lens and viewpoint, not lens alone. These pictures were taken many yards apart; the identical perspectives result from similar camera positioning (David Kilpatrick).*

length. If you stay in one position and photograph the same subject with a wide angle, a standard and a telephoto, you will see that the object is smaller in the viewfinder with the wide angle than it is with the standard, and larger with the telephoto.

People often say that changing focal length affects the perspective in a scene, but this is not correct. The apparent perspective in a scene (the spatial relationship between the objects in it) is actually made to look different by changing the distance from lens to subject. For example, if you point a wide angle lens at a middle distance subject so that it stands 10mm in height in the middle of the frame, and then replace the lens with a telephoto and move yourself back until the same object stands 10mm high in the frame again, you will notice that the relationship between the subject and its surroundings appears to have been quite dramatically altered, causing a quite different visual effect to the wide angle shot. The change in perspective was brought about by moving the camera further from the subject, not by changing the lens.

The visual effects of angle of view and perspective can be used to your advantage to create

*The same object can be photographed with two different lenses from different distances, but occupy the same space in the picture. The perspective is changed because of the alteration in camera distance.*

impact or atmosphere in a picture, and once you begin to understand the visual language of lenses, you can really begin to use their special characteristics to make dynamic and powerful pictures.

## Lens Types

Not so long ago, it was common for most well equipped photographers to carry with them 28mm, 35mm, 50mm, 135mm and 200mm lenses, but then they used to breed them tough in those days! Those five bulky lenses can now commonly be found neatly packaged as two compact zoom lenses, weighing far less than the total weight of the old fashioned five. AF cameras and zoom lenses are very much a part of the same photographic philosophy of flexibility and convenience, and it is a safe bet that most AF SLRs will be used with a zoom lens.

Fixed focal length lenses still have their use however, although the old argument about the optical quality of zooms being inferior to that of fixed focal length lenses is really no longer valid. Zooms are not usually quite as sharp as ordinary lenses, but the difference is very hard to discern unless you go in for huge enlargements.

*The focusing range of AF zooms is important. The 75-300mm AF zoom used by Shirley Kilpatrick for this close-up has continuous focusing down to 1.5 metres even at 300mm focal length.*

# ZOOMS vs OUTFITS

Greater lens speed is one of the major advantages of a single focal length lens. Speed in this context means the maximum aperture of the lens, the larger the aperture, the greater its light passing capabilities. Many zoom lenses have a maximum aperture of about *f*4 at the telephoto end, and *f*3.5 at the wide end. Fixed lenses of the same focal length are often two and sometimes three stops wider than a zoom, which means that they can be used to take pictures in a wider range of situations and conditions.

There are several kinds of lenses for special uses such as photomacrography, sport, wildlife and fisheye photography. These are fixed focal lengths, because their unusual optical design characteristics would make it impractical to incorporate them into zoom configurations. Some zooms do have special features, such as 'macro'. These are fine for getting a closer than normal shot, but cannot be compared with a true macro lens, which will usually provide a life-size magnification of the subject on film.

Special fast telephoto lenses are the favourites of sports and wildlife photographers. Their very large maximum apertures mean that the screen is bright for pin-point focusing and the lens can be used effectively in the poor lighting conditions that often prevail with this type of subject. However, very fast lenses need a lot of very expensive glass, so you have to pay the price for extra quality, in terms of extra weight to carry as well as cash. Super wide angle or fisheye lenses are sometimes used just for their weird visual effects, but they are a very expensive gimmick. Usually, they come into their own in the field of architectural or industrial photography when a shot has to be taken in a confined space.

All these specialist lenses are available in AF systems. But for even the most critical of photographers, who do not have a specialist need, the zooms will provide excellent quality, along with economy and convenience.

Each system will have its own particular zoom ranges, but most will have the close equivalent of a 28 to 80mm and a 70-200mm. These two lenses will cover just

*A 28-80mm zoom and 70-200mm make a complete outfit for most photographers.*

*Not every photographer needs a specialist lens like this 300mm F2.8*

about all your photographic needs. If both together are beyond your budget, a single 35-105mm zoom will provide you with a good degree of flexibility and control.

## Summary

Traditionally, certain focal lengths are used for particular subjects. For example, landscapes are often shot with wide angle lenses, and portraits are normally shot through a short telephoto, such as a 90mm, for a tight crop on the head and shoulders with the camera far enough away for a pleasing perspective. There are good reasons for these traditions, but like all rules they are just asking to be broken. Lenses are the eyes of your photographic system, and it pays to remember that it is what they see that ends up on the film.

Learning to see photographically is partly a process of learning to see in the way your lenses do. When you look at a scene, try to think how that scene would best be translated onto film through a particular focal length of lens. Above all, don't be too lazy to experiment. If you have a zoom lens fitted, there is certainly no excuse for not composing the shot in a variety of ways, at several focal lengths. Exploring in this way will certainly open your eyes to more creative possibilities, and it will soon become second nature to see pictures through your lenses, rather than through your eyes.

# 6: FLASH

*Flash units for AF cameras may be built-in or built-on with a low profile (top left); separate and high in power, with bounce facilities (right); or specialized like this Canon ring flash (bottom left).*

MANY photographers simply think of flash as something to use in an emergency, when there just isn't an alternative, but the new breed of AF SLRs should help to dispel that myth once and for all. Flash is a very versatile light, and can be used to help out in many tricky situations, as well as the traditional 'indoors at parties'. It can be used discreetly with natural light, or boldly to create exciting effects, but whichever way you use it, the new auto systems guarantee to make it extremely easy.

One of the most interesting developments in autofocus SLR design has been the inclusion of built-in flash units. Compact 35mm viewfinder cameras have had built-in flash for years, and like many of the innovatory features that first appeared in the compact, integral flash has finally got to the SLR.

Built-in flash has the great advantage of portability, and you will find that you are far more inclined to use the facility if it is always at hand. Some people find the prospect of carrying around a flashgun as well as a camera and lens a little off-putting. However, having a small programmed unit handy is well worth the effort, as today's flash systems are very easy to use.

*To make sure that pictures taken at 15 or 20 feet come out correctly exposed, flash programs often ALWAYS use apertures like ƒ2.8 or ƒ4 when the lens permits. The results with close-ups may not be good.*

They have been designed as an integral part of your AF photography, to help you deal with many common and difficult lighting problems, indoors and out.

Programmed flash is as simple to use as a programmed exposure mode. You simply pop up the flash if it is built in, or fit the unit onto the hotshoe, and leave the rest to automation. The system sets the correct synch speed and chooses a suitable aperture, and the camera's TTL meter tells the unit when the subject has had enough light. Flash programs tend to use larger (wider) apertures than normal.

## Daylight flash

Most people only think of using flash at night, and yet there are many times in daylight that flash can be very useful. Manufacturers have assessed the type of limitations that affect film and exposure systems in dealing with some tricky lighting situations, mainly backlit scenes, and have developed metering and programmed flash systems to deal with them.

If you have a flash in the hotshoe in programmed mode, or a built-in unit, many AF cameras will automatically assess backlit subjects and deliver the exact

*Many AF SLRs offer programmed synchro-sunshine fill in flash. In daylight, especially backlight, you can switch the flash on and the camera will balance the exposure as above. Photo by Chris Dickie.*

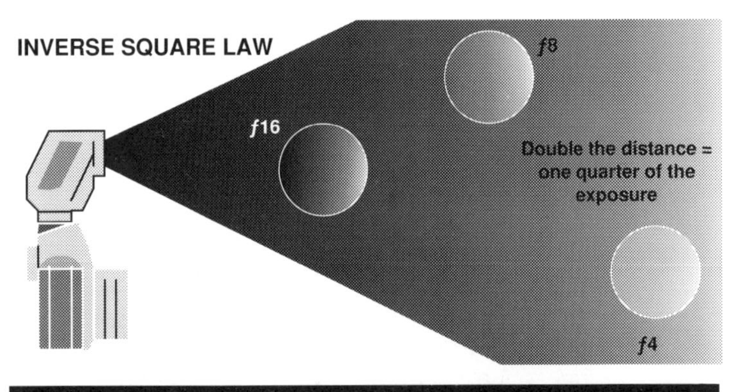


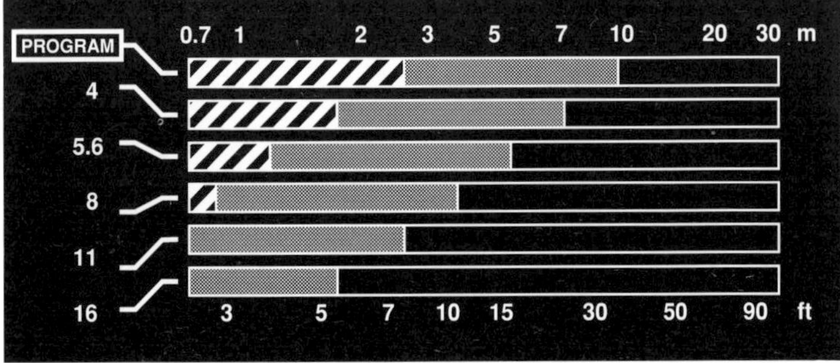


*To understand programmed flash on AF cameras, you have to grasp the Inverse Square Law (top diagram). This states that if you double the distance, you need four times the exposure. On a typical AF program flash (above diagram and right-hand photograph) the end of the tinted bar show the furthest limit of exposure at each f-stop. Program mode selects f2.8 or the widest available lens aperture in order to allow correctly exposed pictures 10m/30ft away, although for a shot 7ft away you might prefer to use f11 with manual flash.*

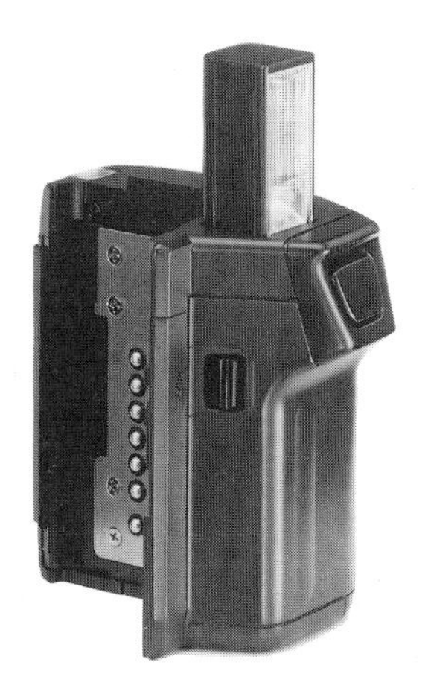

*With the very low power pop-up flash built in to this Olympus handgrip, the wide aperture on program control is advisable in any case. Low power units like this are ideal for family snaps and outdoor fill-in.*

amount of flash to balance any strong backlighting, and thus provide good detail where there would have simply been a silhouette.

Think of all the situations where your portraits in particular have been ruined due to under exposure caused by bright light from behind the subject; on the beach, against a white wall, against a snowy landscape, a window, or the skyline. Those situations are very popular, mainly because to the naked eye they look as though they might make a very good shot.

However, the results are so often disappointing. While the scene looks good to the eye, film just cannot cope with the contrast between the bright background and the darker foreground.

Experienced photographers would tackle this type of lighting situation manually, taking several exposures at varying apertures to ensure a safe shot. Now it can be done automatically with great success. Automatic fill-in flash can clean up the shadows in these situations, and the results are an interesting combination of lovely backlighting, and cleanly lit foreground. The camera solves the whole problem by assessing the various intensities of light around the subject. If the light

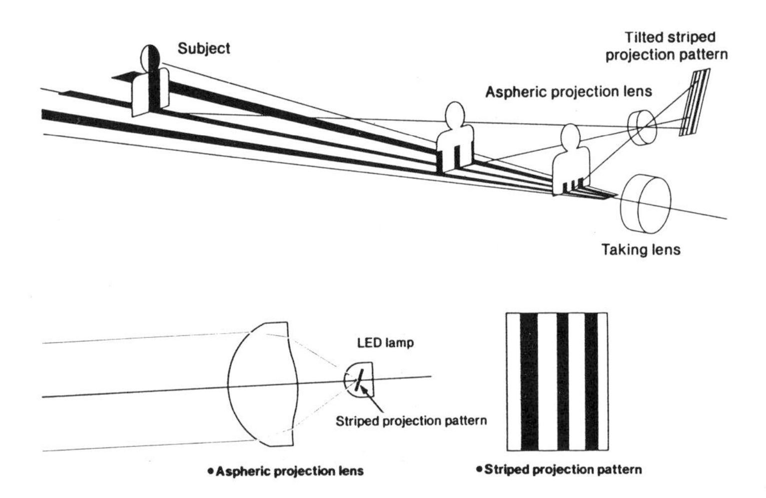


*A pattern of invisible infra-red light can be projected to assist focusing.*

from behind is much stronger than the light from the centre of the scene, i.e. the subject, the flash comes in and cleans up for you, giving just enough flash light to balance the contrast and provide a natural illumination.

## Flash assisted focus

As we have stated earlier, AF systems need a certain degree of contrast in the scene in order to work accurately, so when the light gets so dim that it is hard for the human eye to focus, your AF system will certainly begin to falter too. However, many AF cameras link the focusing system with flash to make photography possible even in total darkness.

Most AF systems use the flashgun, built-in or otherwise, to act as a source of pre-illumination for the AF system to focus on. In some cases, a series of infra-red beams, and in other cases rapid flash bursts, are emitted by the flash unit to form a pattern of light on the subject and help the AF system. Using these methods, the AF SLR fitted with flash makes photography in complete darkness quite easy, a feat which would previously have been almost impossible for the majority of photographers.

## Basic flash technique

Although flash is without a doubt useful for fill-in against a variety of brighter backgrounds, it can also be used with slower than normal synch speeds to allow darker backgrounds to 'burn-in'.

*Ordinary battery-powered flashguns are capable of creative lighting when small areas are involved – this industrial shot by David Kilpatrick used a single Minolta 2800AF flash on an extension cable.*

*A single flash unit on an extension cable can create excellent lighting effects with good modelling and use of light and shade. A spare tripod is useful to support the flash. Photograph by David J. Hatfull.*

*On-camera flash produces flat but detailed portraits marred by hard-edged shadows. It works best against a dark or distant background for snapshots.*

Sunsets or night-time city skylines make great backdrops for dramatic flash lit portraits, and you'll find a flash mode on most AF cameras to allow you to create this type of effect easily.

Using the same system of slower than normal synch speed with flash will allow you to get much more detail into your indoor shots. Black backgrounds are the common result of indoor flash photography, but the sophisticated AF flash modes allow you to capture far more background detail, and thus create a more natural picture.

Built-in flash has many advantages, but it can't offer anything like the flexibility of a hotshoe-mounted gun. Cameras with built-in units also have hotshoes, so they can be upgraded to perform as well as any other camera in this respect. One of the major features of a good flashgun is the ability to direct the angle of its light output. Built-in units can only fire forward, but many top mounted units have swivel and bounce heads. This means that the unit can be pointed upwards, or to the side of the camera, allowing light to be bounced from a wall or ceiling onto the subject.

The benefit of directing the light onto the subject in this way lies in the quality of light you can create. Light from a small flashgun is quite intense and harsh, causing very bright highlights, and very few shadows for moulding features. A much softer and more flattering light is created when a larger light source is used, preferably not from directly in front of the subject.

By reflecting the light from a wall or the ceiling, you are increasing the distribution of light onto the subject, in effect creating a larger, less intense light source. You will be losing some of the light, but the camera will in most cases read the light from the subject through the lens, and so will automatically compensate for any light loss by increasing the flash duration accordingly. By attaching a suitable cable, the flash can even be used off the

*Holding the flash on a cable at arm's length gives stronger modelling but worse shadows.*

*A reflector card opposite the flash greatly improves the result (a small light room also works).*

*Bounce flash off a ceiling softens shadows, but creates dark 'tired eyes' with no sparkle.*

*A twin-tube flash adds a less powerful direct flash which brightens the eyes considerably.*

*A flash bounced off a card at arm's length (45°) is a much better general portrait light.*

*A special diffusing box which covers the flash entirely produces an even softer result.*

*A second flash on an extension cable, mounted behind the sitter, gives attractive hair-lighting.*

*Two direct flashes, at 45° and obliquely to the rear of the sitter, provide ideal male lighting.*

camera, to create more sophisticated lighting effects.

Another common feature of better flash units is the zoom head facility, which allows you to adjust the covering power of the flash to suit the angle of view of the lens in use. Some cameras do this internally and automatically, while others require you to adjust the head manually in or out on a scale from 28mm-90mm or thereabouts.

Traditionally, 1/60 second is the shutter speed for use with flash. Increasingly these days the synch speed is much faster, with one AF SLR allowing synchronization with its own special flashguns at any speed up to 1/2000 second. Some of the more powerful guns for AF cameras can do all kinds of tricks, including shooting five individual bursts in a second. Used with a long exposure, this feature produces stroboscopic effects. These are particularly interesting when used with a subject in motion, such as an athlete going through a routine, or a bird in flight.

One or two units offer the choice between synchronization by the leading blind of the shutter or the trailing blind. In brief, the usual result of photographing with flash and a slow shutter speed is for any moving light sources to appear to be going in the wrong direction.

By using the trailing or second blind as the trigger for flash

*Trailing blind flash synch*

exposure, any light trails stream out behind the subject, giving a more dynamic result. Some units have an extremely rapid recycle time too, which allows you to use the flash with a motor drive for action shots indoors.

## Summary

Once you have taken in all the advantages of flash and AF together, you will probably get into the habit of having the flashgun on the camera at all times, that is if you don't have one of the built-in types. In designing these cameras, the manufacturers were determined to make it possible for absolute beginners to take pictures in all those situations that normally result in disappointment. Mastery of flash has often been the skill which has distinguished the professional from the amateur, but with the advent of these highly intelligent AF flash systems, yet another barrier to consistently successful photography for everyone has been pushed aside.

# 7: FILM CHOICE AND USE

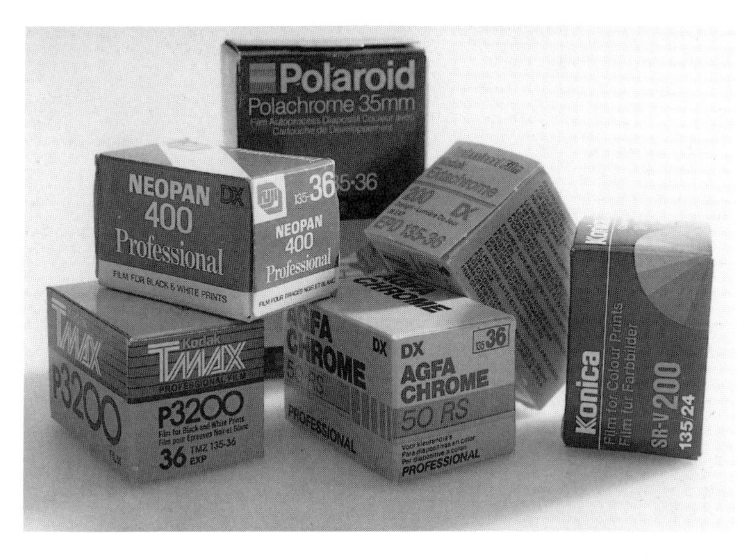


*Which film do you need? In this photo you will find black and white, colour print (negative) and colour slide (reversal) films. Make sure you buy the right type, filmspeed, and number of exposures.*

A CAMERA and lens is only as good as the person who uses it, and the film used in it. You can spend a fortune on the latest AF SLR, but if you use cheap or inadequate film and second-rate processing, you might as well have bought an old box camera. After the operator, film and processing are the weakest links in the chain of successful photography, but a good film used in the right way can add as much to the quality of your pictures as a good camera and lens. It is very important to choose the right kind of film for the conditions, subject and results intended – regardless of make.

## Choosing a film

There are so many films to choose from these days, that no one would blame the inexperienced photographer for getting a little confused when confronted by those shelves full of multicolored boxes at the photographic dealer's. You can always ask a dealer to recommend a film for your specific needs, but if you would rather decide for yourself, just ask yourself some simple questions.

For example, do you want black and white or colour? Unless you have a specific use for black and white, or you want to

*In bright sunshine, with colour and sharpness the most important factors in the picture, Peter Lester chose the slowest slide film possible to ensure the best results – helped by a static subject and a tripod.*

try your hand at developing and printing, then colour is probably what you need. Having said that, black and white photography is considered by some to be more suitable for certain subjects, and it is certainly a very useful process to learn if you are really keen to understand the fundamentals of photography.

The second question to ask is, do you want prints or slides? Print film is usually a little more expensive, as it has to be developed and then printed, slide film is simply developed. You can pass prints around and put them in albums, and you won't need to buy any special viewing apparatus to enjoy them.

Slides do need to be projected onto a screen, or looked at through a viewer. Although this might sound inconvenient, they can look quite spectacular, and you can easily have prints made from slides if you have one or two that you particularly like.

The third important variable is film speed. This is expressed as an ISO number, commonly from ISO 25 through to ISO 400 and occasionally beyond. The higher this number , the more sensitive the emulsion, and consequently the less light it will need. Many photographers choose an average speed film of ISO 100 or 200 to

*For this detail lit by sunlight through a church window, a medium-speed film with the ability to cope with contrast and allow hand-holding in slightly lower light levels was the best choice.*

try to suit as many lighting levels as possible. If you know that you are going to be shooting in very bright sunlight, then a slow film might be best, or if you know that the light could be quite poor, then go for a faster one.

Film length and colour balance are two other considerations you might need to take into account. If you do not use a great deal of film, or you only want to shoot a few frames in poor light at an indoor athletics meeting for example, then get short lengths – 12 , 20, or 24 exposures. For economy, 36 exposure lengths are best, but don't buy a 36 exposure film if it takes you three months to use it all up.

Most film is designed to give natural colours in daylight and with electronic flash, so when daylight-balanced films are used under artificial lights, odd colour casts can occur.

There are special films balanced for tungsten light, which will give acceptable colours under normal household or studio lighting. Tungsten balanced emulsions normally come in the form of slide films, as colour print films are more tolerant of different colour balances, and they can easily be corrected during printing. Slide films are the final

*In winter, at sunset, David Kilpatrick deliberately chose an ISO 400 black and white film to be able to use fast shutter speeds and capture action despite the low light-levels.*

article, and so they need to be correct at the time of exposure.

## Personal taste

After answering those questions, you will probably decide upon something like an ISO 200 colour print film in a 24 exposure length balanced for daylight. At this point all you then have to do is decide which brand you would like, and once again you are faced with a very wide choice. Films certainly vary a good deal from brand to brand, in the way in which they represent natural colours, and in the degree of contrast and fine detail that they can cope with.

There has not been a film invented that will accurately portray natural colours, but there are some that do a better job of it than others. Some of the most popular ones show the world in bright, cheerful colours that are not really accurate at all, but are certainly very appealing to the eye. Others might look less vibrant, but really are quite 'natural' while others have particular colour 'casts', such as brown or blue; a predominance of which appears in what should be neutral areas, such as tones of grey, or skin colours.

There probably isn't a single

*Faced with the need for pictorial quality and a good tonal range, but equipped with only a single hand-held flash to light a large dark flour mill, David used ISO 250 black and white medium-speed film here.*

*Fast film comes into its own for natural light portraits like this strong close-up by Chris Dickie. The grain, clearly visible when enlarged to this size, does not spoil the effect; the colours are pleasantly soft.*

*Chris used ISO 1000 colour slide film for this picture. He also made sure that he took the shot at the closest focus possible on his 50mm standard lens, and avoided any distracting details in the background.*

film that can be described as perfect in every aspect, but everyone finds a favourite sooner or later. Choosing one to suit your taste means experimenting a little with several films to find one that has a colour balance that appeals to you, along with a good tonal range and a degree of sharpness acceptable for the speed of the film. It is well worth the effort to try four or five different brands of the type of film that you have decided is the most useful to you. Just buy a different film each time you need one, always take them to the same reputable processor, and then compare the results carefully.

When you compare them try to choose pictures from each film that have been taken in quite similar daylight conditions, and possibly of similar subjects, so that you can pick out the differences accurately. You will see that some brands show more detail, others have less information in the shadows and highlights, and there will be a general variation in colour from brand to brand. Based on this comparison, you should be able to choose a film that is both accurate and appealing to your eye.

Once you have chosen a film that suits your taste and your type of photography, and a lab that gives accurate and consistent results, you can use them time after time without worrying what the results will be like. As time goes by, you will be able to predict what you can and can't do with that particular film, and so make the necessary allowances when you are taking the picture. Standardizing your procedures in this way is the professional approach, and one way of always getting the results that you want.

## Film speed

It won't be long before you get curious about what all those other films have to offer, and you'll want to put the ISO 200 colour print film to one side and try experimenting with some slower or faster films, and perhaps see what slide films have to offer too. Every film emulsion has its limitations, and its advantages, and as you become more experienced, you will come across situations that demand the use of specific types of film. There is nothing more frustrating than trying to adapt the wrong film for the job, so try to think ahead and decide which is the best film to use if you are going to shoot a particular subject.

### Slow film : ISO 25 – 64

The major characteristics of slow film is very fine grain, which allows every tiny detail of a subject to be recorded, and huge enlargements to be made without losing the fine quality. The colour saturation of slow film is usually very rich indeed, which

*If you are interested in trying still life, slow film between ISO 25 and ISO 80 will be your best choice – along with a tripod to keep the camera steady during long exposures. Photo by David Kilpatrick.*

coupled with the superb detail possible makes it an excellent film for majestic landscapes, colourful plant and animal studies, and architectural photography.

Contrasty lighting does cause problems with slower films, as highlights and shadows sometimes lack detail, so care is needed when assessing a subject for exposure, if you want to record a wide range of tones. If in doubt, bracket your exposures in half-stop steps.

*Important: Be prepared to use a tripod if you are setting out to use very slow film with natural daylight or tungsten studio lights.*

### Medium speed: ISO 80 – 250

Designed to deal with a range of conditions, from bright sunlight to overcast but not dull lighting, medium speed offers a good tonal range, with fine grain, and good colour balance. Medium speeds are excellent for portraits, as they are usually flattering to skin tones, and not so sharp that they will reveal every hair and wrinkle on the face. These are average films, meant to accommodate the widest possible range of subjects and lighting conditions. They are particularly useful with lenses that have a wide aperture, to allow the continued use of the film when the sky gets a little overcast. Even a medium speed film with a very slow lens (*f*4 or *f*5.6) tends to become a bother in all but the brightest lighting, especially if you want to use the long end of your zoom without a tripod.

### Fast films: ISO 320 – 1600

The slower films in this group have good enough colour saturation, and fine enough grain to use for general purposes, especially if you don't need to enlarge the prints over 10 x 8. So if you frequently use the long end of your zoom lens, and you only ever have enprints, then an ISO 400 film will probably suit your general needs. Any of these faster films is suitable for capturing action subjects, or for use indoors under dim lighting or even outdoors at night under bright city centre lighting.

The very fast films have quite noticeable grain, and the colours look a little less realistic. You can use the softer, muted feel of these films to great effect however, for romantic, impressionistic portraits or landscapes, or for gritty urban scenes. Very fast slide films may depend on special processing for their performance and are actually modified versions of ordinary ISO 400 types.

### Ultra-speed films: ISO 2000+

The fastest conventionally processed films are ISO 3200, and may be considered to be much like ISO 1600 materials (in colour negative form for prints). The only film faster than this is made in black and white, and requires extended processing – but can achieve speeds of ISO 25,000 and even ISO 50,000 though this is not recommended. Speeds of ISO 6400 are more commonly used with this type of film, which is available mainly to professionals for sports photography.

## Use and storage

Film cassettes come already marked with a DX code which the camera can often read via simple contacts to set the film speed for the metering system. Just like any other perishable item, film has a sell by date, which is marked on the box but not the cassette. You can often buy out dated film cheaply, and if it has been kept in perfect conditions, it should be quite capable of providing good results for a year or so after its recommended shelf life is up.

Amateur films vary a little from professional ones. The former are designed for a long shelf life, and they are quite forgiving of less than perfect storage conditions. However, you should try to avoid keeping films, in or out of the camera, away from high temperatures and humidity. Don't keep a film in the camera for months on end, and once it

*When you get back from holiday, your pictures should be as colourful and bright as this. If not, you may have stored your film for too long in the heat – or had it X-rayed too often at airports.*

has been exposed get it processed as soon as possible.

Professional films should have even greater care taken over them. They leave the factory in expectation of being used in a very short time, so if you buy films designated as professional, it will be clearly marked on the box. Store them in the fridge, and don't load them unless you are going to shoot the lot quite quickly. If you are going to leave half the film in the camera for a while, keep the camera out of the sun, and away from heat. Exposed films should be processed as soon as possible, and kept cool between times.

The fast films, and particularly ultra-speed films, should not be passed through airport X-ray machines (the official warnings advise against putting any film of ISO 1000 or higher through the machine). They are also more sensitive to heat, ageing and poor processing than other films.

Don't be fooled by all the various enticements which processing labs offer to get their hands on your film. What you want is quality, and consistency – fancy wallets, discounts and speedy service are all very well, but it is the pictures that count. Start off with a well-known service recommended by others who have used it, and only try lower-cost or unfamiliar sounding operators when someone recommends them or shows you good results.

## Summary

There is a film to suit every subject, every type of lighting, and every photographer's tastes, but you will never know if you have found the one that suits your style until you have tried a few out, so never be miserly with film.

In general, print film is easier to use, as it is more forgiving in terms of wrong exposures. Slide film has to be within 1/2 a stop either way to be acceptable, while print film can be up to 2 stops out – two settings on the aperture ring, or the shutter speed dial, before real problems set in.

Slides are capable of brilliant results, and they make a great impression when projected, perhaps with a synchronized soundtrack, or simply seen through a good viewer. You can also have excellent quality prints made from them, and slides are probably easier to print if you are thinking about making your own colour enlargements.

Most of us are on a tight budget these days and film is not a cheap item, especially when coupled with processing, but it is not a good idea to buy a film just because it is cheaper than the better known brands. Stick to the best brands, and find a reputable processing lab. Cheap processing can ruin all the good work you have done, so don't be tempted by discounts and special offers, use the best of both items whenever you can.

# 8: ACCESSORIES

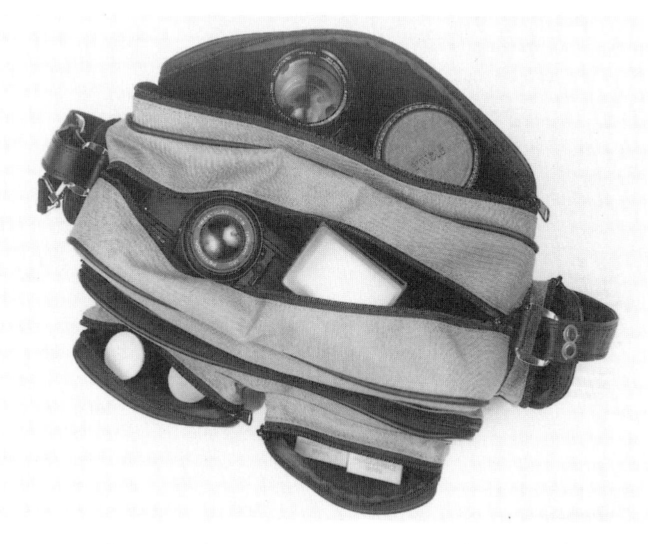

*Even a small camera bag can contain a range of lenses, film, filters, close-up attachments and perhaps a pocket tripod or camera clamp. All these things help make photography easier.*

THERE are two broad categories of accessories; the ones dedicated to the camera's system, and other generally useful gadgets suitable for any SLR camera. No SLR system worth the name comes without a glittering array of add-on extras. Most of them are attractive items to own, and each one has a useful function, but remember that something is only useful if you really need it.

Many people get into photography through an interest in something quite different, such as hiking, bird watching, or historic architecture. Photographers with specialist interests like these often need specialist equipment, such as certain types of lenses, film, or one of those interesting looking close-up gadgets that you often see at the back of the catalogue.

Most of us can get by with just the basics, but there are important accessories that everyone should own, not necessarily a part of the camera's system, but vital nevertheless.

*Photograph overleaf: the average AF SLR has the potential to take this photograph – but not without extras. Peter Lester needed a tripod and a set of extension tubes to enable very close focusing.*

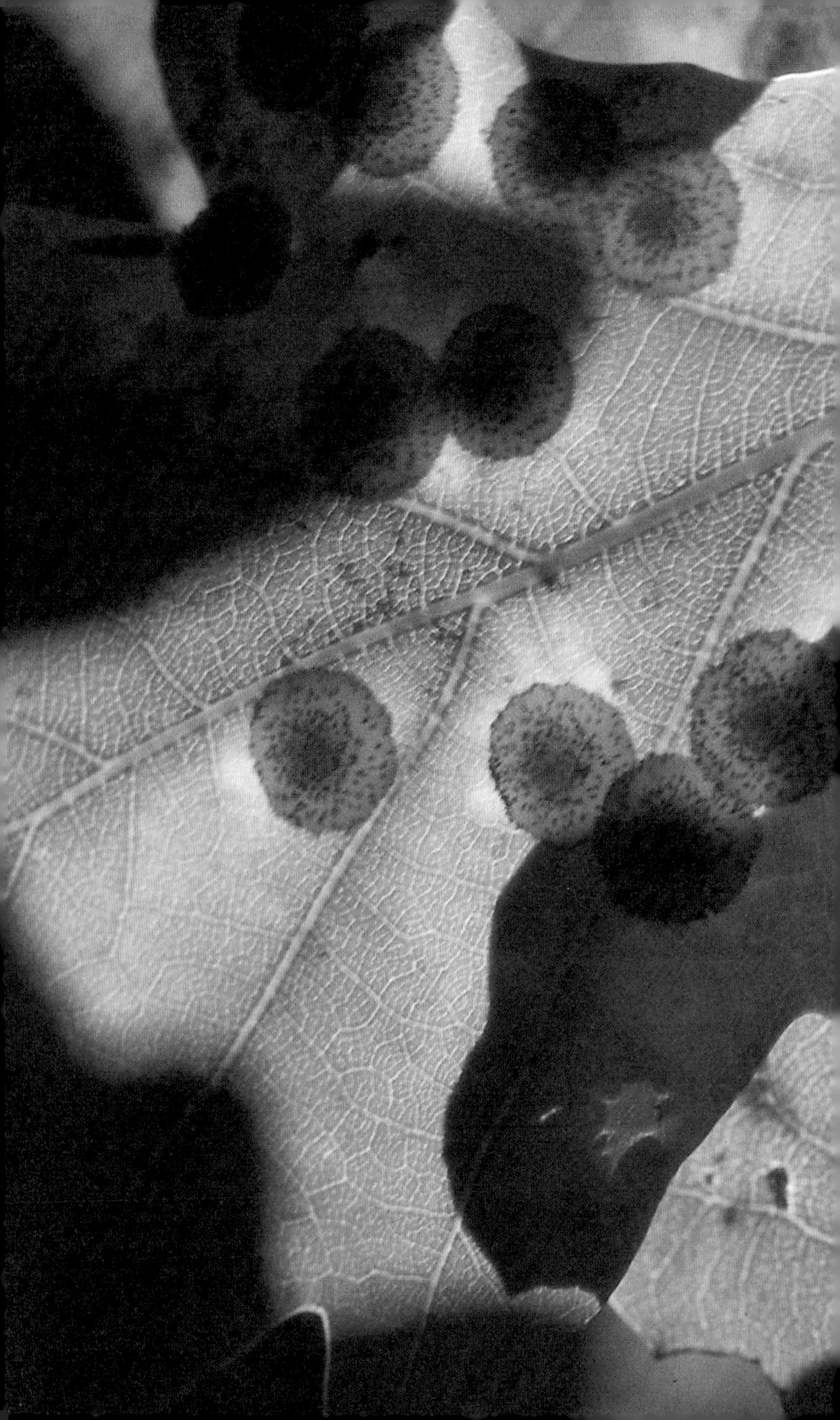

*This unusual accessory from Minolta is a Still Video Back which converts the camera to a video camera storing its pictures on computer disks instead of film.*

## System Accessories

Manufacturers like to make their cameras as useful to as many people as possible, including scientists and specialists. To this end, they make a range of accessories to enable the camera to be used comfortably and effectively in a variety of non standard situations. The following is a small selection of little add-on extras that sometimes make life more bearable and photography more effective.

• **Motor drives:**
Some cameras have built-in film advance motors which can give you quite a rapid firing rate, but, if you want continuous firing for really fast action subjects such as motor racing, then a motor drive will probably come in handy. These fit to the base of the camera, adding weight and bulk, but they will enable you to shoot at up to five frames per second.

• **Viewing screens:**
On the more advanced cameras, viewing screens can be swapped to accommodate special types of subject requirement. Some screens have grids etched onto them to help accurate positioning of subjects, while others are totally plain to allow a completely

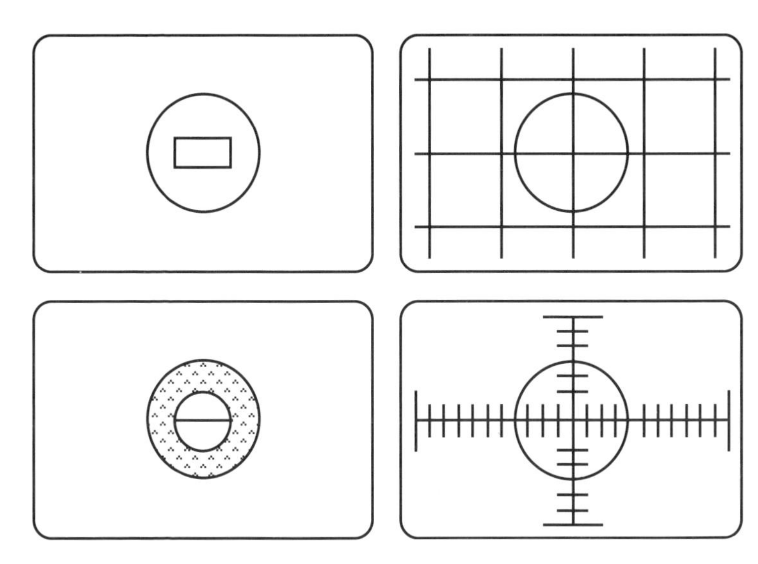

*Above: viewing screens – plain with AF target (standard), matte with grid (for architecture and to aid composition), microprism/split image (for manual focusing) and matte with reticle scale (for scientific uses).*

unobstructed view of the subject.

• Right-angle adapters:
If the camera is to be used for copying, or any other subject in which the eyepiece becomes difficult to view through, such as a low level close-up, a right-angle adapter may help you to see through the viewfinder without twisting your neck into an uncomfortable angle.

*A right-angle finder makes viewing with the camera at bench or ground level easier.*

**• Eyesight Correction:**
Many photographers have to wear glasses, which they find can cause difficulties when using the viewfinder. Odd reflections and scratched spectacle lenses are

*This Technical Data Back can record the exposure details on each frame of film as well as the date and camera used. Most Data Backs only record the date; some control the complete camera system.*

two of the commonest problems. Eyesight correction lenses can be slipped over the viewfinder eyepiece, and form a substitute for your spectacles.

• **Lens Hoods:**
Stray light hitting the lens from obtuse angles can cause a general degradation of the image (flare). Colour saturation and contrast tend to be eroded by flare, which can be prevented by using a lens hood. These are simply metal or rubber tubular or specially-shaped baffles that are fitted to the front of the lens and cut out stray light from outside the lens's angle of view.

• **Data backs:**
These devices offer a range of facilities for specialist or everyday photography. The primary function is to print a short string of data onto your negative or transparency, either in the corner or along the short edge of the negative. You can record the time and date that the picture was taken, the frame number and even the taking aperture and shutter speed, and a personal filing code with some backs.

Some of the more sophisticated backs are programmable, and they can offer facilities such as pre-set starting time for an exposure. All you

*With and without a lens hood – top, the effect of flare from a light source just outside the picture area. Bottom – the 100mm f2 AF lens was fitted with a hood to cut it out. Photographs by David Kilpatrick.*

have to do is enter the time you want the exposure to be made on the control panel, position the camera, and leave the camera to make the exposure at the appointed time. You can even programme some backs to take several exposures at the same time, several at timed intervals, and a set of bracketed exposures too if you like.

All these facilities are excellent for scientific or technical studies, and they are useful too for time-lapse sequences, of landscape or natural history subjects. If you are interested in wildlife photography, many AF cameras also have infrared remote releases, which will allow you to trigger the shutter from a distance, when the subject has come within the field of view of the camera. With the camera locked into the right mode, and the auto-wind facility in operation, you can take several exposures of the subject as it moves around in front of the camera.

## General accessories

After a while, photographers accumulate a tool kit of items that they find useful for aiding their photography, and most find that they just can't live without some little gadget or other. The most useful of these gadgets for most photographers is a tripod or a monopod. As discussed in a previous chapter, camera shake is still one of the most common causes of dissatisfaction with the final image, so do seriously consider using a tripod when the light is poor, when you are using a telephoto, or when using a very small aperture or slow shutter speed.

Tripods come in as many forms as cameras, so here is a quick run-down of the features to look for:

• Legs: these come in round tubes or 'U' section. The round is the most inflexible and usually the strongest, but sometimes the heaviest. Legs telescope into either two or three sections, the three section types usually being the most compact for carrying. To be of real use, a tripod should extend to at least the height of your eye level, but any form of support is better than none at all, so don't worry if you can't afford a really tall one.

• Heads: the part that the camera sits on, these vary quite a lot too. Pan-and-tilt heads are the commonest. These usually have a long handle that twists to lock the base plate into which the camera is screwed. The baseplate tilts up and down and through 90° to allow the camera to be used in vertical format. A locking ring or a knurled screw controls the pan movements which allow the baseplate to be swung around a full 360°. Some have separate pan, tilt and levelling handles.

The other most common head

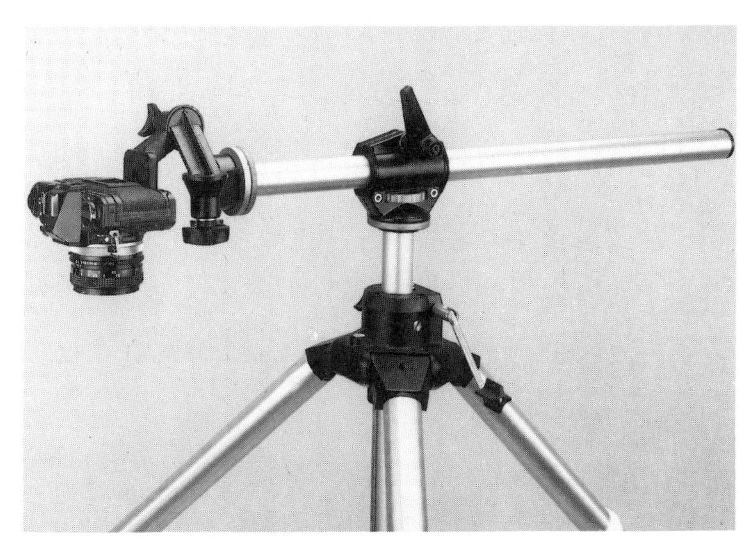

*Top: a useful feature on this tripod is an extension column which allows the camera to be held over flat subjects. Bottom: many tripods are very compact and allow a wide height range.*

*Rubber feet help keep your tripod photography quiet in churches, where flash is often banned. Many historic sites do not allow tripods but will allow camera clamps and monopods.*

is a ball and socket joint, which allows the camera to be infinitely adjusted in any direction, with just one control for all movements. The latter type is often found on more expensive tripods.

• Locks: twist grips, flip locks and screws are the three popular leg locks. Twist grips take the longest to tighten and loosen and are the least easy to use when your hands are cold. Screw locks usually have cumbersome heads which catch on things but are very effective and easy to handle, while flip locks rattle sometimes which is annoying when you are carrying them, but they are very quick to use.

• Feet: look for feet that can be used effectively indoors and out. Some have spikes, others have rubber bungs, others have both. Hard plastic bungs slide about on hard, smooth floors, so choose rubber for general use, and simply take them out if you are photographing on soft ground, and jam the tube into the earth.

• Boom: if you want to do close-up work, a boom arm or tilting centre column that will let you get the camera down to the subject will come in very useful.

*Close-up lenses are ideal if you own a tele zoom already. A +1 close-up lens lets you focus on 1 metre or less, regardless of the lens you have – and 1 metre with a 75-300mm zoom (above) is very close.*

• Monopods: these are simply a single, retractable leg which will still provide quite good support. These are very portable, and so are quite often used by sports photographers who use them longer lenses.

## Close-ups

There are many ways of getting closer to your subject, to make same size or magnified pictures. For autofocus SLRs you will probably have to use the system's dedicated accessories if you want to retain all the auto functions of the camera, so be sure to find out about availability and compatibility of close-up equipment when you buy the camera.

• Close-up lenses: these are the cheapest close-up accessory, a screw-in magnifying lens that attaches to the front of your taking lens like a filter. These offer a useful degree of magnification, but some are not of the best optical quality.

• Extension tubes: these move the lens away from the camera's body, consequently enlarging the image focused on the film plane. They come in various sizes, and can be used in multiples to get

*Very few AF systems include bellows, as autofocus is not practical with them. These Novoflex bellows have adaptors to fit most makes; here a special Minolta 25mm ultra-close-up lens is being used.*

magnifications of up to 1:1, but they do need to be strictly compatible if auto functions are to be maintained.

• Bellows: an infinitely variable extension tube, on a rack and pinion focusing bed. These can be quite expensive, but used with a macro lens, they can provide extreme close-ups.

## Summary

Whenever possible, travel light when you go out to take pictures, but do think about putting together a small tool-kit of useful accessories. Accessories soon accumulate when you get into a specific subject, or a particular way of taking pictures. However, for general use, a compact tripod is always handy, as is a lens hood for each of your lenses. Flash is something that we have already discussed but is it worth mentioning again, as is a small gadget bag with good access, to carry everything in.

You may also find a few extras like a pocket torch, a film leader retriever, a notebook, penknife, cleaning cloth and blower-brush, spare batteries and a polythene bag to cover the camera during light rain will make photography simpler in difficult conditions.

# 9: FILTERS

*Round screw-in filters are very compact and can be stacked together, with end caps, for storage. The filters from camera makers (left) are usually much slimmer than cheaper independent ones (right).*

MANY people never use filters and are perfectly happy with the results of their photography, but it is well worthwhile investigating the use of one or two for everyday use. The purpose behind filters is twofold, either to make the picture look more like 'real life', or to change the image to make it look completely unreal.

They do this by altering the nature of the light coming into the camera, which means in effect that there is less light coming in through the lens. However, the camera's metering system will cope with any changes that the filters have on the intensity of light.

## Filter systems

• Round filters: these screw into the front of the lens. The disadvantage is that not all your lenses will have the same size filter thread, so you will either have to buy a different filter for each lens, or just restrict the filter to use with your lenses which take that particular size. Some makers do try to standardize on the filter size for all their lenses, which is a selling point to professionals who tend to use a lot of filters. The advantage of round filters is that you don't need to buy any holders or other devices to use them, and some

*Square filter systems, above, require more storage space but each filter can be used with every lens you own, regardless of filter fitting, as long as you have an adaptor ring and a master filter holder.*

lenses can be adapted to match your principal filter thread by using step-up or step-down rings.

• Square filters: these need special holders, which fit onto the front of the lens. The square filter is simply slotted in; more than one can be used if required. Adaptor rings can be bought which allow the holder to fit a wide range of filter threads, making this type more adaptable than round types. Your filters won't become obsolete if you change your camera system to one with a different thread size. Very large filter threads require professional size square filters.

## Black and White

If you decide to have a go at black and white photography, filters will probably become quite important to you. Black and white film sees the world as densities of tone, and represents everything as shades of grey. Unfortunately film has its limitations, and some colours are represented in lighter or darker

*Right: the square filter system is very well suited to graduated filters, which can be slid up or down to shade in the sky area precisely. Photograph by Chris Dickie.*

*A landscape shot without a filter on FP4 black and white film has a very boring sky with no tones to speak of – the blue sky records as plain white, hardly any darker than the clouds.*

tones than they would appear to the eye. Filters help to provide a more natural balance of tones in certain circumstances. They block out some wavelengths of light but let others pass through. A Haze/UV filter only blocks out invisible rays which cause distant haze and can be left fitted all the time as an 'optical lens cap.'

Light, as you probably know, is made up of different colours which you can see clearly when it is broken down into its constituents by a prism, or by droplets of water in the air when a rainbow is formed. Film is more sensitive to some of these colours than others. Hence what looks quite bright to the eye as a coloured object may appear duller than you expected as a grey tone.

Black and white film is particularly sensitive to blue, which often results in skies looking far less dramatic on your black and white print than they did in the original scene. The addition of a yellow filter will block out some of the blue, resulting in a darker tone for the sky. Progressively more dramatic effects can be achieved with orange and red filters. With a red filter, which blocks out almost all the blue wavelengths, the blue sky will appear almost black.

*A yellow filter has little effect on exposure, but improves the shot considerably (top). For real drama, a red filter (bottom) creates rich dark skies and requires a +1 correction to most SLR exposure systems.*

## Filters for colour

Colour film is balanced to provide natural colours in certain types of light. However, some lighting conditions affect the way in which colour will be recorded on film, but this can be adjusted by using the right filters.

For example, some situations can result in colour film recording an overall blue cast, especially in areas of neutral colour, such as skin or white clothing. This often happens on an overcast day, in snow scenes, near the sea, and even on sunny days in the shade. The problem is exaggerated by some brands of film that have a tendency towards 'coolness' in their colour balance.

• Common coldness: to overcome the tendency of all films to coldness in neutral areas of your picture use a skylight filter, which you can leave on at all times. This is usually called a 1A, and it has a slightly pinkish tinge.

• Blue casts: these can be prevented by warm-up filters, which are designated 81A. They are warmer still, and if you use them in normal daylight you will find that everything has a yellow tinge to it, so don't leave one on at all times.

*Previous page: a polarizer deepens the blue sky on colour shots just as red does with b/w.*

• Red casts: sometimes lighting situations occur that cause a very strong reddish cast in the picture. Most people don't mind this as much as they do the blue cast, as the red looks warm and flattering. However, you can prevent the cast by using a pale blue 82A filter.

• Green/orange casts: artificial light causes most problems; fluorescent lights cause a green tinge which makes people look positively ill, while tungsten lights – i.e. normal household lights – make everything look very orange. The orange cast can be prevented with an 80A blue and the green by using an FL-D, which is a magenta filter.

## Polarizer

There is one filter that is useful for black and white or colour photography, and that is a polarizing filter. Glare reduces colour saturation and tonal density, and reflections from shiny surfaces can also make a picture look untidy. A polarizing filter reduces glare, allowing the subject's colour to be recorded naturally. Irritating reflections can be removed by rotating the polarizing filter to the right angle. These filters are very good for creating really deep blue skies and for capturing the true colour of the sea or other highly reflective surfaces.

Most autofocus SLRs use an

*Another use of the polarizer is to cut out unwanted reflections or surface glare. The top picture is taken without a polarizer; the only change for the bottom shot was to fit and rotate a polarizer.*

*The difference between sunlight (top) and overcast light (bottom) is considerable in colour terms. To correct this, an 81A filter can be used; it will not make the sun shine, but the result looks 'warmer'.*

*Peter Lester fitted a soft focus filter – usually reserved for portraits – to diffuse the forms and colour in this woodland scene. Do not hesitate to experiment with filters in this way; it often pays off.*

internal beam-splitter or semi-silvered mirror for the focusing or metering systems – perhaps for both. Ordinary 'linear' polarizers can cause problems with these systems, resulting in difficulty in focusing (through loss of light) or inaccurate meter setting. You should always specify a circular polarizer – this refers to its technical performance, not its shape – rather than a linear polarizer. Never just fit the old polarizer you had with your previous camera system.

## Special effects

There is a huge range of special effects filters which can transform a subject in many different ways.

• Graduated filters: these are coloured in the top half only, with the colour gradually fading to plain glass about half way down. They are commonly used to put a colour into the sky, and can be quite useful if the scene is interesting but the sky is very bland. Colours range from pale blue and grey, to bright green or purple. Use with discretion.

• Star bursts turn any point light source, such as a candle flame, into a choice of star points from four to sixteen depending on the filter. They usually soften the picture a little too.

• Soft focus: make everything look misty, and pastel coloured. They are often used to photograph wedding portraits and other romantic situations.

• Novelties: there are filters that do some very strange and often rather tacky things, such as the rainbow filter which has a solid looking rainbow dyed into it which you can position somewhere apt in a landscape, yucch! Prism filters offer a multifaceted view of the subject, three or five repeated images of the same person or view on a single frame. There is even one which provides a kind of speed blur which can be positioned behind a moving, or indeed a stationary subject.

## Summary

Special effects filters are only useful if they add something to a subject. Many people use them as an end in themselves, but the results are usually terrible. Filters are extremely useful for 'fine-tuning' your film to suit the changing light conditions outdoors and in, especially if you are using transparency film, which can't be adjusted during printing as can negative film. Be careful when using very thick filters, such as a polarizer or the square filter types, with wide angle lenses. The frames can sometimes actually be seen by the lens at very small apertures, which will result in the corners of your pictures being cut off.

# 10: PICTURE POINTS

*The world through the viewfinder is different from the world through your eyes – the frame is selective, and the camera lens enhances the perspectives and geometry of nature. Photograph by David Kilpatrick.*

GREAT photographs don't leap out from behind bushes demanding to be taken, they have to be made. Successful photographers use their knowledge of their equipment to alter and refine the subject to create a more visually effective result. They use all the visually exciting qualities of the subject, or its surroundings, to create as much interest and impact as possible in the picture.

Spotting the best visual qualities of a scene or subject, and being able to emphasize them by means of your equipment, comes with experience. To help you start thinking along the right lines, imagine how the following methods of picture building might apply to the kind of photographs that you like to take.

## Composition

What you see in the viewfinder is more or less what you will get in your finished picture, so use every part of the viewfinder as you would a canvas if you were a painter. When it comes to imposing that rectangular frame around a group of objects, a person or a scene, take your time and look at the entire area of the scene through the camera. Ask yourself if everything you want is

*A composition works best when there is nothing in the frame expect the subject (above). Small focal points, even right at the corners of the shot, always attract attention (opposite). Photographs by Peter Lester.*

there in the composition within the viewfinder frame, and also ask yourself if there is anything there that you don't want.

Watch out for unwanted objects creeping into the edges of the frame. If there are irrelevant items intruding, move yourself to a different position, get closer to the main subject, use a longer lens, adjust your height or even get the subject to move if you can. Remember that what you see in the viewfinder is what you get in the picture, and everything that appears in a picture takes on equal importance.

For example, you are shooting a head and shoulders portrait in your living room, and you are just concentrating on getting the expression right and have not noticed the lampshade hovering in the background over the sitter's head like a hat. In the picture everything that is more or less in focus gets equal attention, so while the lampshade might be 'invisible' to the naked eye, in the picture it will appear as dominant as the person innocently posed under it.

## Focus

Cluttered backgrounds also make poor compositions, as they detract from the foreground

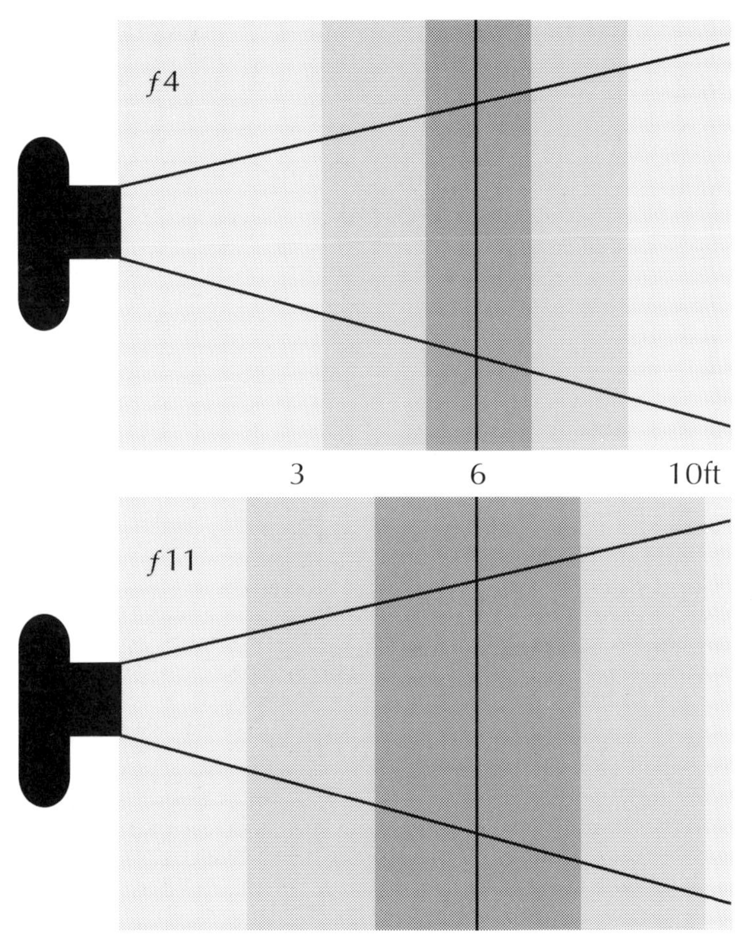


*Depth of field (the extent to which sharp focus extends in front of and behind the exact point of focusing) depends on lens aperture. Here the darkest shaded area shows visually sharp detail, the medium shading soft but recognisable detail, and the light area visually blurred detail. Some AF SLRs have a depth-of-field preview device which allows you to see this effect on the viewing screen at the 'working aperture' which the lens will be set to for the final photograph. The viewing aperture (full aperture) always shows the minimum possible depth of field.*

subject which you probably wanted to be the main interest. Giving an object or a person the main emphasis in a picture can be done in many ways, but doing it through selective focus is perhaps the most flexible, and effective way of dealing with cluttered backgrounds, or even foregrounds. Selective focus means focusing on the single most important part of the picture, and throwing out of focus as much as you can of the surrounding area, particularly the background, by using restricted depth of field.

Depth of field, you will remember, is the area of ground in front of and behind the subject that will also be sharp when the subject is sharply focused. There are two important points to remember when using focus creatively. These are that the size of aperture used affects the depth of field, and so does the lens to subject distance affect the depth of field. The wider the aperture you choose, and the closer you are to your subject, the narrower will be the depth of field.

Shooting a portrait indoors can often result in a lot of unwanted clutter in the background, but if you shoot with the lens almost wide open, from the right distance, you will see in the viewfinder that when the head and shoulders are in focus the background is just a blur. You can use this technique to single out anything of interest from its surroundings, providing you can get the right aperture and distance combination for the lens you are using.

## Deep focus

Other subjects can be given emphasis by being sharp from the foreground to the horizon, for example a picture with a figure in the foreground gazing out to sea at a sailing boat. In this case the distance from lens to subject is again important, as is the size of aperture used. If you are too close to the foreground, you will not be able to get the distant part of the shot in focus as well. You will need to use the very smallest aperture that you can to ensure maximum depth of field.

In the case of deep or narrow focus techniques, a depth of field preview button will come in very useful. This is simply a lever or button which stops the lens down to the aperture selected for your exposure, giving you a preview of which parts of the picture will be in focus and which will not.

The focal length of lens chosen will have an effect on the effectiveness of the technique. For narrow focus shots a standard to telephoto lens is more effect-ive, and for deep focus a wide angle. AF SLRs all have a choice of exposure modes, at least one of which will be suitable for creative use of apertures. Make sure that you are in the right mode for experimenting with focus.

*Top: at f2, the standard 50mm lens has very limited depth of field. Both foreground and background detail is blurred. Bottom: the same shot, stopped down to f22, is sharp throughout its depth.*

*Top: a 24mm wide-angle at f8 produces a photograph which is sharp from foreground to infinity, like the 50mm at f22. Bottom: a zoom set to 210mm at f8 has just as little depth of field as the 50mm at f2.*

## Shutter speeds

Choosing the right speed to avoid camera shake is very important, and some cameras help you to do just that. However, don't simply resign the shutter to the role of keeping your pictures sharp. The shutter is also a creative tool, just as the aperture is. You can use a fast speed of 1/250th and more to freeze action for effect, or you can use slower speeds to allow parts of the subject to blur. Both techniques can add creative interest and impact to your pictures.

For example, ask yourself which looks the more attractive and realistic, a waterfall in which the flow of water has been completely arrested by a fast shutter speed or one in which the water is a blur of white and blue. It is really a matter of taste, but either way of shooting the picture can be attractive. The eye does see rapid movement as a blur of colour, so for a realistic effect it is sometimes better not to stop all the action. Remember though that if you do use a slow shutter speed you are risking camera shake, which means that everything could end up blurred. So for long exposures to create blur, use the camera on a tripod. This will ensure a good contrast between the blurred movement and the sharp stationary items. For speeds around 1/30 or even 1/15 a firm surface to rest your elbows on may be enough.

## Creative control

Almost every feature and facility of the camera can be used as a creative tool to alter the scene to suit your own perception of it. Every permutation of aperture, shutter speed, exposure mode and focal length can provide a creative result that you can control. Familiarizing yourself with your equipment will certainly lead to better pictures. However, good pictures don't stem just from the skilful use of equipment. Experienced photographers learn to use light, colour, pattern, shape and scale to add impact and interest.

• Contrast: think about visual contrasts between rough and smooth, light and dark, in colour, in size and scale, in age, in style, in mood, in shape, or in angle. Elements such as these offer visual stimulation to the viewer, and make your pictures more dynamic.

• Texture and pattern: almost every scene or object has an innate visual quality, which can be used to effect in a picture. Patterns occur in nature and all around us in our cities and the countryside. Patterns can be an interesting subject in themselves, or they can simply be used to emphasize or add to another part of the picture. Breaking such a pattern can produce a strong visual effect.

*The appearance of flowing water can be greatly improved by using a tripod and selecting shutter priority with a speed of between 1/8 second (used here by David Kilpatrick) and 1 second.*

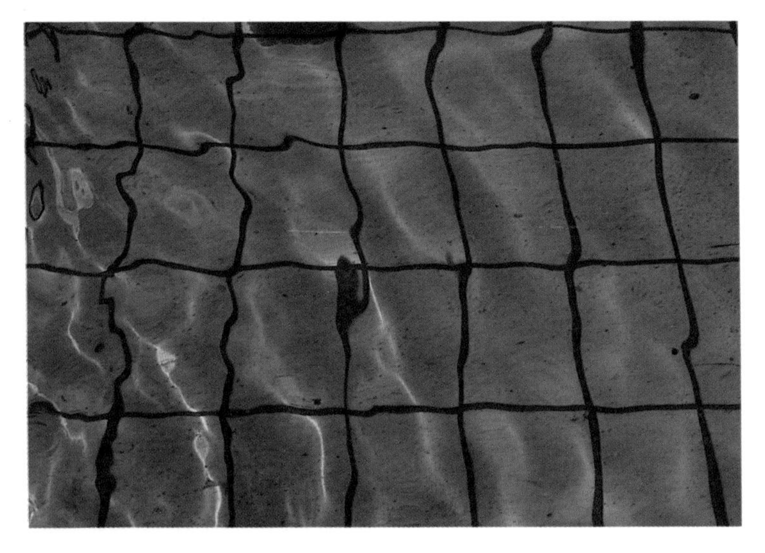

*Pattern shots can be found wherever natural or man-made designs repeat themselves (above); texture is best brought out by the right lighting at a sharp angle (right). Photographs by Peter Lester.*

• Texture: this is strongly affected by the angle of lighting in the shot and the actual size of the light source. At 12 noon on a bright but overcast day, with the whole sky acting as a diffused light source, the shadows are very weak and every detail of a surface is revealed, which makes it excellent lighting for smooth surfaces. Low angle light in a clear sky throws harsh black shadows, giving rough surfaces a very gritty feel to them.

• Colour: everyone uses colour film these days, but does everyone exploit the excitement and atmosphere that colour can provide? As you probably know, certain colours have almost symbolic or psychological connotations. For example, red is warm, black is sinister, yellow, bright blue and green are very jolly, grey is sad. Remember how colour can affect the feel of a picture and use this fact to add a mood or statement.

• Light: the quality of light and how it affects a subject is often the most important creative element in a picture. Light affects mood and atmosphere just as colour in a subject does. Dull grey days, when there is little sun and not much colour, look sad;

*A day of bad weather does not mean a day without good photographs – look for breaks in the clouds, shafts of sunlight, and underexpose for dramatic results. Photograph by David Kilpatrick.*

bright sunny days, when colours glow, look happy. Soft, diffused light is flattering, quiet and gentle. Harsh, direct light is dramatic and even sinister. Light changes with the time of day and with the weather. Watch how changing light affects the landscape. Try to use the drama of light, indoors and out, to enhance your pictures.

## Summary

Beyond the realm of the snapshot is a whole new world of creative photography. Once you have mastered the controls of your AF SLR you can begin to use your knowledge to control the image, creating pictures in the style that you like, saying things with pictures that you want to say. With experience, you will become more visually aware through photography. Then, when you begin to 'see photographically', the world will become one big photographic subject. You will recognize the inherent beauty that lies within even the most everyday item. Look around you, watch how the light affects colour, texture and mood. Make sure that you arrange all these exciting scenes effectively and with clarity in the viewfinder.

# 11: IDEAS AND SUBJECTS

*Photography begins at home – or at least with the family. Chris Dickie captured a superbly natural moment which also formed an excellent composition (original in colour).*

THERE are many more different things to photograph than there are people to photograph them. You can divide the most commonly photographed subjects into broad categories, such as landscape, portraits and so on. Under these broad headings a huge range of interpretations and techniques are possible, and there are just as many ways of photographing a landscape or a portrait as there are photographers.

The following is a selection of popular subjects, with some advice about the best techniques to use, and some ideas on how to approach them a little differently. However, don't forget that you are taking pictures to please yourself. These ideas are simply suggestions to get you started.

## Families / Children

Most people who wouldn't dream of calling themselves photographers take pictures of their family, and especially their children, quite regularly. Many photographers get their first experience with this particular subject, and go on from there to develop a serious interest. However, when they go on to be 'serious' photographers they tend to neglect the family as a subject.

This is a shame, because there really is endless scope for excellent pictures here, so don't relegate your family to the realms of the snapshot, take them seriously.

When taking pictures for the family album be as careful as you would with any other subject. When taking group pictures, arrange the sitters into a good composition. A tripod is handy for this as it enables you to leave the camera in position while you move people about to get the best composition in the viewfinder. Watch out for intrusive backgrounds if you are shooting people indoors – remember your selective focusing techniques.

Outdoors, get sitters to pose with their backs to the sun so that their eyes are not all screwed up. Watch out for harsh shadows across the face, under the eyes and nose. This is the ideal time to use fill-in flash to brighten up the shadows and balance out the strong light coming from behind the subject.

Watch out for opportunities to photograph family activities; dad at work, kids at play, mother's hobby, school sports day, holidays, outings, parties, weddings and homecomings. And don't just make a record of these events, use the opportunity to make some excellent photographs. You probably know your own children too well; other people may often appreciate your pictures more than you do.

*Top: looking into the sun produces bad expressions. Use backlighting (bottom).*

*A good background does not have to mean a plain wall or an empty lawn. It is much better to show your family or children in a real scene which may be remembered in future.*

*A candid portrait taken in an active situation is nearly always better than a static pose. A fast film and medium telephoto lens allowed David J. Hatfull to shoot this concert portrait without using flash.*

## Portraits

There are two basic types of portrait; the formal studio shot using flash or tungsten light, and the candid, informal portrait, sometimes taken with the co-operation of the subject but frequently without. You do not need a real studio to take formal portraits. You can make your own background out of an old sheet or paper, and position it so that the lens sees simply that and the sitter. Paint spray cans are excellent for creating blobs of two or three different colours all over the background. When photographed out of focus these blobs become diffused and blended and can look extremely attractive. Don't forget to light the background as well as the sitter. To do this you can use two tungsten studio lights or two flash units with long synch cords.

Flash and tungsten studio lamps can cause harsh shadows on the face, so experiment with bouncing the flash, and using reflectors. A reflector can be any white, flat object, such as a large polystyrene tile. Use this to reflect light onto the shaded side of the face by positioning it on the opposite side of the model from the main light source. Get an assistant to move it about while you look through the viewfinder and assess what happens to the highlights and shadows.

Flash is harder to position as you can't see it until you fire it,

*For a formal portrait, use a plain background and soft lighting. Studio flash helps control this.*

although studio flash heads do have modelling lights. If you don't want to use flash or studio lights, you could use the natural daylight coming in through a window or skylight, again using the reflector to fill in shadows and balance extreme contrast.

Informal portraits are often more descriptive of character and usually, more visually interesting. A zoom lens is invaluable for pictures of people on the move as it allows you to crop tightly without moving yourself. More importantly, it allows you to frame a good composition without demanding too much co-operation from the sitter.

*Landscapes provide opportunities for small scenes as well as open views. Above: fungi by flash, under trees. Right: autumn provides a strong monochromatic theme. Photographs by Peter Lester.*

For this type of picture try to include something of the sitter's environment. Consider them not just as a head and shoulders, but as a figure in a setting; a setting that has something to say about the subject. Think carefully about composition, colour, texture and all the previously discussed pictorial qualities in the surroundings, and use them to make the picture and the sitter more appealing, and the photograph more interesting.

## Landscapes

Surely one of the most popular subjects, and yet the most badly photographed, is landscape. The major problem is lighting, followed closely by viewpoint. By far the least interesting quality of light is that to be found at midday in the middle of summer. On a sunny day the light from directly overhead casts no shadow and so contours and shapes in the landscape are utterly flat and featureless. Yet this is often the time of day when most people take landscape photographs.

Mornings and late afternoon are far better for landscape photography. The low angle of light reveals textures, models shapes, and creates dramatic

*Landscape shots need positive attitudes to composition; use figures, paths, roads, streams or natural features to lead the eye into the scene and give it scale. Photograph: David Kilpatrick.*

shadows across the land; the sky becomes richer in colour and clouds look more interesting. Changeable weather, with the resulting shafts of sunlight from behind stormy clouds, misty mornings, or mellow, warm lit evenings are much better lighting conditions for landscape pictures with visual impact.

Too many landscapes are also spoiled by being vague, general views, full of tiny details that are far too small to be interesting. Look for dynamic shapes, patterns and prominent features in the landscape, and use these natural designs to make interesting compositions. Try and get something into the shot that will provide a sense of scale, a figure, a building or a tree for example. Lead the eye into the picture with gradually receding elements, or perhaps a road or river meandering into the distance.

## Architecture

Towns and cities are full of pictures waiting to be taken. Architecture offers a wealth of material for the keen eyed photographer, although getting good pictures of buildings is not always easy. It is often hard to find a good position from which to photograph in order to get the

*Architecture does not have to be formal; there is no need to photograph an entire building. Here the contrast between a tree and the lines of church provides a good subject. Photograph: Peter Lester.*

whole building in. However, a very wide angle lens, such as a 24 or 21mm, will enable you to get in most of a four-storey building from across the street.

Time of day and the resulting quality of light also play an important role in successful architectural photography. Early evening is often the best time to take pictures of buildings, when the light is warm and mellow, making the bricks and stone and sometimes even concrete look more attractive. Watch out for interesting reflections in windows, creating contrasts of old and new styles. Use a telephoto lens to pick out interesting details in the buildings, and to compress perspective, and a wide angle to exaggerate the converging vertical lines of tall structures when the camera is tilted upwards.

Indoors use a fast film and a tripod to allow you to capture the lovely atmospheric light, such as that to be found in churches. Watch out for tricky lighting conditions indoors, and use your exposure modes and your metering system carefully. Take at least three exposures of difficult subjects, using your compensation dial or whatever other method is to hand to bracket your first exposure with an over- and an under-exposed shot.

## Travel

More and more people are venturing to distant and exotic locations for their holidays, but even domestic vacation spots can offer excellent opportunities for pictures. Travel shots are usually about people and places that the visitor finds interesting. However, don't be fooled into shooting away at everything you find interesting without considering it as a photograph too. The same rules and techniques of architectural, landscape, and portrait photography apply when on holiday, so think before you turn back into a snapshooter.

Suggestions for good travel photography come under the same general headings as previously discussed. Every location will have its own attractions and difficult local conditions. The following is a general rough survival guide. Always take more film than you imagine you will need, as buying film in some locations is either not advisable due to quality and cost, or simply not possible. Try to keep film cool, never leave it around in direct sun, and don't leave the camera around in the heat either.

Keep sand and sea water well away from the camera. Electronics and sea water do not mix, and sand in the AF motor will sound as bad as it really is. A strongly zipped gadget bag is the best place for a camera near the sea and on dusty journeys.

A lens hood and a skylight filter attached to each lens will protect the front element from dust, flare and the excessive blueness you will find near the sea.

Be careful where you get your camera out in Iron Curtain and Muslim countries. Do not point your camera where it might not be welcome, and try to ask permission whenever possible.

Festivals and local traditions are well worth investigation, and a visit to the local tourist information office is rarely wasted. A trip away from the tourist centres is also a good idea. The countryside just outside many of the most crowded and unpleasant resorts on the Mediterranean is very picturesque, and usually deserted. Read a good travel guide before you leave the country, and put together a loose schedule of places to visit that might offer some good picture potential.

Finally, remember that pictures taken in hot countries at midday are rarely satisfactory for reasons already discussed. White glare is all you'll see in some locations, but a few hours later the colours will be vibrant in the lowering sun. Do as the locals do; get up early to catch local activity around markets or quaysides, go home for a noon siesta, and get out with the camera again when the day has cooled down and the colours have warmed up.

*If you can travel, take your camera. Spectacular scenes are always worth recording, especially from the right viewpoint. Mountain views are best shot from high ground, as here by R. Tandy.*

## Wildlife

Natural history has become a very popular subject in recent years, probably due to the public's increasing awareness of the natural world, helped along by newsworthy environmentalist groups and some brilliant television programmes. Although normally a specialist subject, more and more natural history shots are attempted as people realize the immense potential in nature for images of striking power and beauty.

There is a great deal of specialist equipment available for wildlife photography, but telephoto zooms of around 200mm are quite adequate for large birds and small mammals if you can get reasonably close. Many zooms also feature so called 'macro' which will get you a 1/4 life size close up of plants and insects.

Many wildlife shots are set up following careful study of the creature, its home and feeding habits. Often remote control units are used, along with twin flash set ups, to ensure a well-lit shot. In these circumstances equipment is often introduced slowly, over a period of a few days, so as not to frighten the animal or bird away.

Butterflies and other insects are subjects that anyone can photograph. A 50 or 90mm macro lens, along with a flash unit, are all you need for really excellent close ups of insects. Dull days are best for butterflies, because they don't fly around so much, and the flash will still give you a crisp, colourful picture.

Do try to light the background with the flash as well as the subject, to keep a natural feel to the shot, and don't get so excited by the subject that you forget to pay attention to the composition. Remember that it is still a photograph that you are making, not just a record, so pay attention to details. Use the depth of field preview to check focus if you have time, as close-ups often suffer from being out of focus in the wrong places, and check the shutter speed if you are not using flash, as camera shake spoils many close up shots too.

Butterfly farms present the same problems with humidity and heat that tropical holidays can spring on you; the camera suddenly mists up. When this happens, leave it alone – do not remove the lens or the insides will be affected by similar condensation. Let the camera warm up for half an hour, then try to use it. Professionals visiting zoos often warm the camera on the studio radiator for an hour or two and then wrap it up inside a padded case before setting off.

A tripod really is essential for keeping the camera steady, as small apertures, and consequently slow shutter speeds, often have to be used for subjects such as plants and even trees. Other handy items include an umbrella

*An eye for detail found a frozen leaf, above, for David Kilpatrick's AF 50mm lens. Programmed exposure ensured a fast shutter speed, and the exposure was cut by 1/2 stop using an over-ride dial.*

for keeping the wind off plants that are liable to blow about, flash for fill-in of back lit subjects, or a reflector to brighten up the shadows while keeping a natural feel to the lighting.

## Summary

Photography can easily become much more than just a hobby. Once you have mastered the machine, and learned just what it can do for you, you can concentrate on learning to see. Looking through the lens of your camera will become more and more of a pleasure, as you begin to see the potential all around you for photography. Seen through your camera, the world will become a more visually exciting place, and your eyes will soon learn to see photographically.

Your autofocus SLR will prove to be a genuine companion in this personal exploration of the visual world, and it will continue to offer you good service as your demands grow. Keep this book in your camera kit for a while, and use it if you get a bit stuck. Soon you won't need it at all, but I hope that it will have been of some use to you in getting you started in what may prove a life-long interest in a most rewarding pastime. Happy shooting!

# 12: THE FUTURE OF AF SLRs

*Minolta's Dynax 7000i is the first of a new generation of intelligent AF SLRs which are better able to track moving subjects, identify focusing problems and accept alternative control programs.*

MULTIPLE autofocus and metering sensors in the latest generation of AF SLRs, linked to programmed computer chips, provide a kind of 'intelligence' which allows the camera to track the changing focus of moving subjects. These cameras use the focus values detected by three or more sensor areas to determine where the main subject is positioned in the frame. They can detect potential focus failures such as groups with a gap in the middle.

Predictive focus is a feature which uses the information provided by a focus sensor about the rate of change of focus to work out, in effect, the subject's 'speed'. In reality the system does not actually do this. What it does it to store information about how many times the lens refocuses as you view a moving subject, and what those focus changes are. A typical AF system will detect over 100 separate focus distances with a standard lens, easily enough to plot a simple graph in the computer's memory (figuratively speaking).

When you press the shutter release, the computer in the camera uses this data to continue focusing the lens right up to the moment of exposure. This means that the big failing of AF systems

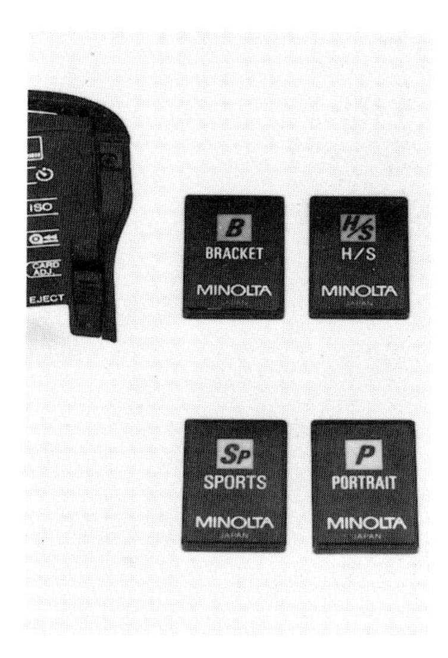


*These slot-in cards are no larger than postage stamps, but change the camera's functions instantly.*

in action photography has been successfully overcome. Predictive focus also works during motor-drive operation, giving much more reliable tracking of a moving subject at several frames per second; the problem with earlier systems has been that each time the mirror dropped down after a shot, the subject had moved so far that the focus needed extra time to catch up, slowing down the sequence rate.

## Expansion cards

New chip technology has enabled makers to design slot-in cards or modules which alter the camera's functions. The selection of programs available on these cards is limited only by the functions of the camera; the most popular cards will probably be those for sports photography, portraiture, and special effects such as changing the focus rapidly during exposure to produce a soft effect.

Professional functions not built-in to the camera to start with, such as exposure bracketing and data storage, can be added by means of cards. These functions have previously been available in AF SLRs, but very often the buyer has had a difficult choice, as no one system offered every feature in the same camera.

Expansion cards, a concept which is completely new to cameras, mean that in future a professional body may consist of a shutter and mirror assembly with nothing more than basic electronics. A change of card (in effect, replacing the circuitry of the camera) will make the camera ideal for studio flash work, outdoor action work, remote control and many other applications – just in the same way that SLRs have always benefited from interchangeable lenses and viewfinders.

Tomorrow's AF SLRs will almost certainly be even more advanced, and the new compact lightweight lenses which are being produced today point the way to compact cameras and outfits no larger than conventional SLRs and lenses.

# INDEX

# INDEX